FROM THE MAKER OF THE TEST

The Official SAT Subject Test Study Guide

Biology

The College Board
New York, N.Y.

About the College Board

The College Board is a mission-driven not-for-profit organization that connects students to college success and opportunity. Founded in 1900, the College Board was created to expand access to higher education. Today, the membership association is made up of over 6,000 of the world's leading educational institutions and is dedicated to promoting excellence and equity in education. Each year, the College Board helps more than seven million students prepare for a successful transition to college through programs and services in college readiness and college success—including the SAT® and the Advanced Placement Program®. The organization also serves the education community through research and advocacy on behalf of students, educators, and schools.

For further information, visit collegeboard.org

Copies of this book are available from your bookseller or may be ordered from College Board Publications at store.collegeboard.org or by calling 800-323-7155.

Editorial inquiries concerning this book should be addressed to the College Board, SAT Program, 250 Vesey Street, New York, New York 10281.

ISBN 13: 978-1-4573-0920-5

Printed in the United States of America

4 5 6 7 8 9   23 22 21 20 19 18

Distributed by Macmillan

Contents

The SAT Subject Tests™

About SAT Subject Tests

SAT Subject Tests™ are a valuable way to help you show colleges a more complete picture of your academic background and interests. Each year, nearly one million Subject Tests are taken by students throughout the country and around the world to gain admission to the leading colleges and universities in the United States.

SAT Subject Tests are one-hour exams that give you the opportunity to demonstrate knowledge and showcase achievement in specific subjects. They provide a fair and reliable measure of your achievement in high school — information that can help enhance your college admission portfolio. The Biology Subject Test is a great way to highlight your understanding, skills, and strengths in biology.

This book provides information and guidance to help you study for and familiarize yourself with the Biology Subject Test. It contains actual, previously administered tests and official answer sheets that will help you get comfortable with the tests' format, so you feel better prepared on test day.

The Benefits of SAT Subject Tests

SAT Subject Tests let you to put your best foot forward, allowing you to focus on subjects that you know well and enjoy. They can help you differentiate yourself in a competitive admission environment by providing additional information about your skills and knowledge of particular subjects. Many colleges also use Subject Tests for course placement and selection; some schools allow you to place out of introductory courses by taking certain Subject Tests.

Subject Tests are flexible and can be tailored to your strengths and areas of interest. These are the **only** national admission tests where **you** choose the tests that best showcase your achievements and interests. You select the Subject Test(s) and can take up to three tests in one sitting. With the exception of listening tests, you can even decide to change the subject or number of tests you want to take on the day of the test. This flexibility can help you be more relaxed on test day.

REMEMBER

Subject Tests are a valuable way to help you show colleges a more complete picture of your academic achievements.

Who Should Consider Subject Tests?

Anyone can take an SAT Subject Test to highlight his or her knowledge of a specific subject. SAT Subject Tests may be especially beneficial for certain students:

- Students applying to colleges that require or recommend Subject Tests — be aware that some schools have additional Subject Test requirements for certain students, majors, or programs of study

- Students who wish to demonstrate strength in specific subject areas

- Students who wish to demonstrate knowledge obtained outside a traditional classroom environment (e.g., summer enrichment, distance learning, weekend study, etc.)

- Students looking to place out of certain classes in college

- Students enrolled in dual-enrollment programs

- Home-schooled students or students taking courses online

- Students who feel that their course grade may not be a true reflection of their knowledge of the subject matter

The SAT Subject Test in Biology is particularly useful for students interested in majors with a focus in STEM (Science, Technology, Engineering, and Math).

Who Requires the SAT Subject Tests?

Most college websites and catalogs include information about admission requirements, including which Subject Tests are needed or recommended for admission. Schools have varying policies regarding Subject Tests, but they generally fall into one or more of the following categories:

- Required for admission

- Recommended for admission

- Required or recommended for certain majors or programs of study (e.g., engineering, honors, etc.)

- Required or recommended for certain groups of students (e.g., home-schooled students)

- Required, recommended, or accepted for course placement

- Accepted for course credit

- Accepted as an alternative to fulfill certain college admission requirements

- Accepted as an alternative to fulfill certain high school subject competencies

- Accepted and considered, especially if Subject Tests improve or enhance a student's application

In addition, the College Board provides a number of resources where you can search for information about Subject Test requirements at specific colleges.

- Visit the websites of the colleges and universities that interest you.
- Visit College Search at www.collegeboard.org.
- Purchase a copy of *The College Board College Handbook*.

Some colleges require specific tests, such as mathematics or science, so it's important to make sure you understand the policies prior to choosing which Subject Test(s) to take. If you have questions or concerns about admission policies, contact college admission officers at individual schools. They are usually pleased to meet with students interested in their schools.

Subject Tests Offered

SAT Subject Tests measure how well you know a particular subject area and your ability to apply that knowledge. SAT Subject Tests aren't connected to specific textbooks or teaching methods. The content of each test evolves to reflect the latest trends in what is taught in typical high school courses in the corresponding subject.

The tests fall into five general subject areas:

English	History	Mathematics	Science	Languages	
				Reading Only	**with Listening**
Literature	United States History	Mathematics Level 1	Biology E/M	French	Chinese
	World History	Mathematics Level 2	Chemistry	German	French
			Physics	Italian	German
				Latin	Japanese
				Modern Hebrew	Korean
				Spanish	Spanish

Who Develops the Tests

The SAT Subject Tests are part of the SAT Program of the College Board, a not-for-profit membership association of over 6,000 schools, colleges, universities, and other educational associations. Every year, the College Board serves seven million students and their parents; 24,000 high schools; and 3,800 colleges through major programs and services in college readiness, college admission, guidance, assessment, financial aid, and enrollment.

Each subject has its own test development committee, typically composed of teachers and college professors appointed for the different Subject Tests. The test questions are written and reviewed by each Subject Test Committee, under the guidance of professional test developers. The tests are rigorously developed, highly reliable assessments of knowledge and skills taught in high school classrooms.

Deciding to Take an SAT Subject Test

Which Tests Should You Take?

The SAT Subject Test(s) that you take should be based on your interests and academic strengths. The tests are a great way to indicate interest in specific majors or programs of study (e.g., engineering, pre-med, cultural studies).

You should also consider whether the colleges that you're interested in require or recommend Subject Tests. Some colleges will grant an exemption from or credit for a freshman course requirement if a student does well on a particular SAT Subject Test. Below are some things for you to consider as you decide which test(s) to take.

Think through your strengths and interests

- List the subjects in which you do well and that truly interest you.

- Think through what you might like to study in college.

- Consider whether your current admission credentials (high school grades, SAT® scores, etc.) highlight your strengths.

Consider the colleges that you're interested in

- Make a list of the colleges you're considering.

- Take some time to look into what these colleges require or what may help you stand out in the admission process.

- Use College Search to look up colleges' test requirements.

- If the colleges you're interested in require or recommend SAT Subject Tests, find out how many tests are required or recommended and in which subjects.

Take a look at your current and recent course load

- Have you completed the required course work? The best time to take SAT Subject Tests is at the end of the course, when the material is still fresh in your mind.

- Check the recommended preparation guidelines for the Subject Tests that interest you to see if you've completed the recommended course work.

- Try your hand at some SAT Subject Test practice questions on collegeboard.org or in this book.

Don't forget, regardless of admission requirements, you can enhance your college portfolio by taking Subject Tests in subject areas that you know very well.

If you're still unsure about which SAT Subject Test(s) to take, talk to your teacher or counselor about your specific situation. You can also find more information about SAT Subject Tests on collegeboard.org.

When to Take the Tests

We generally recommend that you take the Biology Subject Test after you complete biology course(s), prior to your senior year of high school, if possible. This way, you will already have your Subject Test credentials complete, allowing you to focus on your college applications in the fall of your senior year. Try to take the test soon after your courses end, when the content is still fresh in your mind. More information about the topics covered on the Biology Subject Test can be found later in this book.

Because not all Subject Tests are offered on every test date, be sure to check when the Subject Tests that you're interested in are offered and plan accordingly.

You should also balance this with college application deadlines. If you're interested in applying Early Decision or Early Action to any college, many colleges advise that you take the SAT Subject Tests by October or November of your senior year. For regular decision applications, some colleges will accept SAT Subject Test scores through the December administration. Use College Search to look up policies for specific colleges.

This book suggests ways you can prepare for the Subject Tests in Biology. Before taking a test in a subject you haven't studied recently, ask your teacher for advice about the best time to take the test. Then review the course material thoroughly over several weeks.

How to Register for the Tests

There are several ways to register for the SAT Subject Tests.

- Visit the College Board's website at www.collegeboard.org. Most students choose to register for Subject Tests on the College Board website.

- Register by telephone (for a fee) if you have registered previously for the SAT or an SAT Subject Test. Call, toll free from anywhere in the United States, 866-756-7346. From outside the United States, call 212-713-7789.

- If you do not have access to the Internet, find registration forms in *The Paper Registration Guide for the SAT and SAT Subject Tests*. You can find the booklet in a guidance office at any high school or by writing to:

    The College Board
    SAT Program
    P.O. Box 025505
    Miami, FL 33102

When you register for the SAT Subject Tests, you will have to indicate the specific Subject Tests you plan to take on the test date you select. You may take one, two, or three tests on any given test date; your testing fee will vary accordingly. Except for the Language Tests with Listening, you may change your mind on the day of the test and instead select from any of the other Subject Tests offered that day.

Student Search Service®

The Student Search Service® helps colleges find prospective students. If you take the PSAT/NMSQT, the SAT, an SAT Subject Test, or any AP Exam, you can be included in this free service.

Here's how it works: During SAT or SAT Subject Test registration, indicate that you want to be part of the Student Search. Your name is put in a database along with other information such as your address, high school grade point average, date of birth, grade level, high school, e-mail address, intended college major, and extracurricular activities.

Colleges and scholarship programs then use the Student Search to help them locate and recruit students with characteristics that might be a good match with their schools.

Here are some points to keep in mind about the Student Search Service:

- Being part of Student Search is voluntary. You may take the test even if you don't join Student Search.

- Colleges participating in the Search do not receive your exam scores. Colleges can ask for the names of students within certain score ranges, but your exact score is not reported.

- Being contacted by a college doesn't mean you have been admitted. You can be admitted only after you apply. The Student Search Service is simply a way for colleges to reach prospective students.

- Student Search Service will share your contact information only with approved colleges and scholarship programs that are recruiting students like you. Your name will never be sold to a private company or mailing list.

Keep the Tests in Perspective

Colleges that require Subject Test scores do so because the scores are useful in making admission or placement decisions. Schools that don't have specific Subject Test policies generally review them during the application process because the scores can give a fuller picture of your academic achievement. The Subject Tests are a particularly helpful tool for admission and placement programs because the tests aren't tied to specific textbooks, grading procedures, or instruction methods but are still tied to curricula. The tests provide level ground on which colleges can compare your scores with those of students who come from schools and backgrounds that may be far different from yours.

It's important to remember that test scores are just one of several factors that colleges consider in the admission process. Admission officers also look at your high school grades, letters of recommendation, extracurricular activities, essays, and other criteria. Try to keep this in mind when you are preparing for and taking Subject Tests.

Score Choice™

In March 2009, the College Board introduced Score Choice™, a feature that gives you the option to choose the scores you send to colleges by test date for the SAT and by individual test for the SAT Subject Tests — at no additional cost. Designed to reduce your test day stress, Score Choice gives you an opportunity to show colleges the scores you feel best represent your abilities. Score Choice is optional, so if you don't actively choose to use it, all of your scores will be sent automatically with your score report. Because most colleges only consider your best scores, you should still feel comfortable reporting scores from all of your tests.

More About collegeboard.org

collegeboard.org is a comprehensive tool that can help you be prepared, connected, and informed throughout the college planning and admission process. In addition to registering for the SAT and SAT Subject Tests, you can find information about other tests and services, browse the College Board Store (where you can order *The Official Study Guide for All SAT Subject Tests*™ and other guides specific to Mathematics and Sciences), and send e-mails with your questions and concerns. collegeboard.org also contains free practice questions for each of the 20 SAT Subject Tests. These are an excellent supplement to this Study Guide and can help you be even more prepared on test day.

REMEMBER
Score Choice gives you an opportunity to show colleges the scores you feel best represent your abilities.

Once you create a free online account, you can print your SAT admission ticket, see your scores, and send them to schools.

More College Planning Resources The College Board offers free, comprehensive resources at Big Future™ to help you with your college planning. Visit **bigfuture.org** to put together a step-by-step plan for the entire process, from finding the right college, exploring majors and careers, and calculating costs, to applying for scholarships and financial aid.

How to Do Your Best on the SAT Subject Test

Get Ready

Give yourself plenty of time to review the material in this book before test day. The rules for the SAT Subject Tests may be different than the rules for most of the tests you've taken in high school. You're probably used to answering questions in order, spending more time answering the hard questions, and, in the hopes of getting at least partial credit, showing all your work.

When you take the SAT Subject Tests, it's OK to move around within the test section and to answer questions in any order you wish. Keep in mind that the questions go from easier to harder. You receive one point for each question answered correctly. No partial credit is given, and only those answers entered on the answer sheet are scored. For each question that you try but answer incorrectly, a fraction of a point is subtracted from the total number of correct answers. No points are added or subtracted for unanswered questions. If your final raw score includes a fraction, the score is rounded to the nearest whole number.

Avoid Surprises

Know what to expect. Become familiar with the test and test-day procedures. You'll boost your confidence and feel a lot more relaxed.

- **Know how the tests are set up.** All SAT Subject Tests are one-hour multiple-choice tests. The first page of each Subject Test includes a background questionnaire. You will be asked to fill it out before taking the test. The information is for statistical purposes only. It will not influence your test score. Your answers to the questionnaire will assist us in developing future versions of the test. You can see a sample of the background questionnaire for the Biology Subject Test at the start of each practice test in this book.

- **Learn the test directions.** The directions for answering the questions in this book are the same as those on the actual test. If you become familiar with the directions now, you'll leave yourself more time to answer the questions when you take the test.

- **Study the sample questions.** The more familiar you are with question formats, the more comfortable you'll feel when you see similar questions on the actual test.

- **Get to know the answer sheet.** At the back of this book, you'll find a set of sample answer sheets. The appearance of the answer sheets in this book may differ from the answer sheets you see on test day.

- **Understand how the tests are scored.** You get one point for each right answer and lose a fraction of a point for each wrong answer. You neither gain nor lose points for omitting an answer. Hard questions count the same amount as easier questions.

A Practice Test Can Help

Find out where your strengths lie and which areas you need to work on. Do a run-through of a Subject Test under conditions that are close to what they will be on test day.

- **Set aside an hour so you can take the test without interruption.** You will be given one hour to take each SAT Subject Test.

- **Prepare a desk or table that has no books or papers on it.** No books, including dictionaries, are allowed in the test room.

- **Read the instructions that precede the practice test.** On test day, you will be asked to do this before you answer the questions.

- **Remove and fill in an answer sheet from the back of this book.** You can use one answer sheet for up to three Subject Tests.

- **Use a clock or kitchen timer to time yourself.** This will help you to pace yourself and to get used to taking a test in 60 minutes.

The Day Before the Test

It's natural to be nervous. A bit of a nervous edge can keep you sharp and focused. Below are a few suggestions to help you be more relaxed as the test approaches.

Do a brief review on the day before the test. Look through the sample questions, answer explanations, and test directions in this book or on the College Board website. Keep the review brief; cramming the night before the test is unlikely to help your performance and might even make you more anxious.

REMEMBER
You are in control.
Come prepared.
Pace yourself.
Guess wisely.

The night before test day, prepare everything you need to take with you. You will need:

- your admission ticket

- an acceptable photo ID (see page 11)

- two No. 2 pencils with soft erasers. Do not bring pens or mechanical pencils.

- a watch without an audible alarm

- a snack

Know the route to the test center and any instructions for finding the entrance.

Check the time your admission ticket specifies for arrival. Arrive a little early to give yourself time to settle in.

Get a good night's sleep.

Acceptable Photo IDs

- Driver's license (with your photo)

- State-issued ID

- Valid passport

- School ID card

- Student ID form that has been prepared by your school on school stationery and includes a recognizable photo and the school seal, which overlaps the photo (go to www.collegeboard.org for more information)

The most up-to-date information about acceptable photo IDs can be found on collegeboard.org.

REMINDER **What I Need on Test Day**

Make a copy of this box and post it somewhere noticeable.

I Need   **I Have**

Appropriate photo ID   _____

Admission ticket   _____

Two No. 2 pencils with clean soft erasers   _____

Watch (without an audible alarm)   _____

Snack   _____

Bottled water   _____

Directions to the test center

Instructions for finding the entrance on weekends _____

I am leaving the house at _____ a.m.

Be on time or you can't take the test.

On Test Day

You have a good reason to feel confident. You're thoroughly prepared. You're familiar with what this day will bring. You are in control.

Keep in Mind

You must be on time or you can't take the test. Leave yourself plenty of time for mishaps and emergencies.

Think positively. If you are worrying about not doing well, then your mind isn't on the test. Be as positive as possible.

Stay focused. Think only about the question in front of you. Letting your mind wander will cost you time.

Concentrate on your own test. The first thing some students do when they get stuck on a question is to look around to see how everyone else is doing. What they usually see is that others seem busy filling in their answer sheets. Instead of being concerned that you are not doing as well as everyone else, keep in mind that everyone works at a different pace. Your neighbors may not be working on the question that puzzled you. They may not even be taking the same test. Thinking about what others are doing takes you away from working on your own test.

Making an Educated Guess

Educated guesses are helpful when it comes to taking tests with multiple-choice questions; however, making random guesses is not a good idea. To correct for random guessing, a fraction of a point is subtracted for each incorrect answer. That means random guessing — guessing with no idea of an answer that might be correct — could lower your score. The best approach is to eliminate all the choices that you know are wrong. Make an educated guess from the remaining choices. If you can't eliminate any choice, move on.

REMEMBER

All correct answers are worth one point, regardless of the question's difficulty level.

Cell phones are not allowed to be used in the test center or the testing room. If your cell phone is on, your scores will be canceled.

10 Tips
FOR TAKING THE TEST

1. **Read carefully.** Consider all the choices in each question. Avoid careless mistakes that will cause you to lose points.

2. **Answer the easier questions first.** Work on less time-consuming questions before moving on to the more difficult ones.

3. **Eliminate choices that you know are wrong.** Cross them out in your test book so that you can clearly see which choices are left.

4. **Make educated guesses or skip the question.** If you have eliminated the choices that you know are wrong, guessing is your best strategy. However, if you cannot eliminate any of the answer choices, it is best to skip the question.

5. **Keep your answer sheet neat.** The answer sheet is scored by a machine, which can't tell the difference between an answer and a doodle. If the machine mistakenly reads two answers for one question, it will consider the question unanswered.

6. **Use your test booklet as scrap paper.** Use it to make notes or write down ideas. No one else will look at what you write.

7. **Check off questions as you work on them.** This will save time and help you to know which questions you've skipped.

8. **Check your answer sheet regularly.** Make sure you are in the right place. Check the number of the question and the number on the answer sheet every few questions. This is especially important when you skip a question. Losing your place on the answer sheet will cost you time and may cost you points.

9. **Work at an even, steady pace and keep moving.** Each question on the test takes a certain amount of time to read and answer. Good test-takers develop a sense of timing to help them complete the test. Your goal is to spend time on the questions that you are most likely to answer correctly.

10. **Keep track of time.** During the hour that each Subject Test takes, check your progress occasionally so that you know how much of the test you have completed and how much time is left. Leave a few minutes for review toward the end of the testing period.

 **IMPORTANT**

If you erase all your answers to a Subject Test, that's the same as a request to cancel the test. All Subject Tests taken with the erased test will also be canceled.

REMEMBER
Check your answer sheet. Make sure your answers are dark and completely filled in. Erase completely.

7 Ways
TO PACE YOURSELF

1. Set up a schedule. Know when you should be one-quarter of the way through and halfway through. Every now and then, check your progress against your schedule.

2. Begin to work as soon as the testing time begins. Reading the instructions and getting to know the test directions in this book ahead of time will allow you to do that.

3. Work at an even, steady pace. After you answer the questions you are sure of, move on to those for which you'll need more time.

4. Skip questions you can't answer. You might have time to return to them. Remember to mark them in your test booklet, so you'll be able to find them later.

5. As you work on a question, cross out the answers you can eliminate in your test book.

6. Go back to the questions you skipped. If you can, eliminate some of the answer choices, then make an educated guess.

7. Leave time in the last few minutes to check your answers to avoid mistakes.

After the Tests

Most, but not all, scores will be reported online several weeks after the test date. A few days later, a full score report will be available to you online. Your score report will also be mailed to your high school and to the colleges, universities, and scholarship programs that you indicated on your registration form or on the correction form attached to your admission ticket. The score report includes your scores, percentiles, and interpretive information. You will only receive a paper score report if you indicate that you would like one.

What's Your Score?

Scores are available for free at www.collegeboard.org several weeks after each SAT is given. You can also get your scores — for a fee — by telephone. Call Customer Service at (866) 756-7346 in the United States. From outside the United States, dial (212) 713-7789.

Some scores may take longer to report. If your score report is not available online when expected, check back the following week. If you have not received your mailed score report by eight weeks after the test date (by five weeks for online reports), contact Customer Service by phone at (866) 756-7346 or by e-mail at sat@info.collegeboard.org.

Should You Take the Tests Again?

Before you decide whether or not to retest, you need to evaluate your scores. The best way to evaluate how you really did on a Subject Test is to compare your scores to the admissions or placement requirements, or average scores, of the colleges to which you are applying. You may decide that with additional work you could do better taking the test again.

? **Contacting the College Board**

If you have comments or questions about the tests, please write to us at the College Board SAT Program, P.O. Box 025505, Miami, FL 33102, or e-mail us at sat@info.collegeboard.org.

Biology E/M

Purpose

The Subject Test in Biology E/M measures the knowledge students would be expected to have after successfully completing a college-preparatory course in high school. The test is designed to be independent of whichever textbook you used or the instructional approach of the biology course you have taken. The Biology E/M Test is for students taking a biology course that has placed particular emphasis on either ecological or molecular biology, with the understanding that evolution is inherent in both. The test lets you choose the area in biology for which you feel best prepared. If you are unsure of the emphasis in your biology course, consult your teacher.

Format

The Subject Test in Biology E/M with either ecological (Biology-E) or molecular (Biology-M) emphasis has a common core of 60 questions, followed by 20 questions in each specialized section (Biology-E or Biology-M). Each test-taker answers 80 questions.

Content

The content covered in the Subject Test in Biology E/M and descriptions of the topics are shown in the chart on page 18.

Topics Covered

Topics	Approximate Percentage of E Test	Approximate Percentage of M Test
Cellular and Molecular Biology	15%	27%
Cell structure and organization, mitosis, photosynthesis, cellular respiration, enzymes, biosynthesis, biological chemistry		
Ecology	23%	13%
Energy flow, nutrient cycles, populations, communities, ecosystems, biomes, conservation biology, biodiversity, effects of human intervention		
Classical Genetics	15%	20%
Meiosis, Mendelian genetics, inheritance patterns, molecular genetics, population genetics		
Organismal Biology	25%	25%
Structure, function, and development of organisms (with emphasis on plants and animals), animal behavior		
Evolution and Diversity	22%	15%
Origin of life, evidence of evolution, natural selection, speciation, patterns of evolution, classification and diversity of organisms		

How to Prepare

Before you take the Biology E/M Test, you should have completed a one-year course not only in biology but also in algebra so that you can understand simple algebraic concepts (including ratios and direct and inverse proportions) and apply such concepts to solving word problems. Success in high school biology courses typically requires good reasoning and mathematical skills. Your preparation in biology should have enabled you to develop these and other skills that are important to the study of biology. Familiarize yourself with directions in advance. The directions in this book are identical to those that appear on the test.

Skills Specifications	Approximate Percentage of Test
Knowledge of Fundamental Concepts:	30%
remembering specific facts; demonstrating straightforward knowledge of information and familiarity with terminology	
Application:	35%
understanding concepts and reformulating information into other equivalent forms; applying knowledge to unfamiliar and/or practical situations; solving problems using mathematical relationships	
Interpretation:	35%
inferring and deducing from qualitative and quantitative data and integrating information to form conclusions; recognizing unstated assumptions	

You should be able to recall and understand the major concepts of biology and to apply the principles you have learned to solve specific problems in biology. You should also be able to organize and interpret results obtained by observation and experimentation and to draw conclusions or make inferences from experimental data, including data presented in graphic and/or tabular form. Laboratory experience is a significant factor in developing reasoning and problem-solving skills. Although testing of laboratory skills in a multiple-choice test is necessarily limited, reasonable experience in the laboratory will help you prepare for the test.

Notes: (1) You will not be allowed to use a calculator during the Biology E/M Test.

(2) Numerical calculations are limited to simple arithmetic.

(3) The metric system is used in these tests.

How to Choose Biology-E or Biology-M

- Take Biology-E if you feel more comfortable answering questions pertaining to biological communities, populations, and energy flow.

- Take Biology-M if you feel more comfortable answering questions pertaining to biochemistry, cellular structure and processes, such as respiration and photosynthesis.

- Indicate choice of Biology-E or Biology-M on your answer sheet on test day.

You can decide whether you want to take Biology-E or Biology-M on the test day by gridding the appropriate code for the test you have chosen on your answer sheet. *Only questions pertaining to the test code that is gridded on your answer sheet will be scored.*

Note: Because there is a common core of questions, you are not allowed to take Biology-E and Biology-M on the same test date. You can take them on two different test dates.

Score

The total score for each test is reported on the 200 to 800 scale.

Sample Questions
Classification Questions

Each set of classification questions has five lettered choices in the heading that are used in answering all of the questions in the set. The choices may be statements that refer to concepts, principles, organisms, substances, or observable phenomena; or they may be graphs, pictures, equations, formulas, or experimental settings or situations.

Because the same five choices are applicable to several questions, classification questions usually require less reading than other types of multiple-choice questions. Answering a question correctly depends largely on the sophistication of the set of questions. One set may test recall; another may ask you to apply your knowledge to a specific situation or to translate information from one form to another (descriptive, graphical, mathematical). The directions for this type of question specifically state that you should not eliminate a choice simply because it is the correct answer to a previous question.

The following are directions for and an example of a classification set.

E/M Core Section (Ecological and Molecular)

Directions: Each set of lettered choices below refers to the numbered questions or statements immediately following it. Select the one lettered choice that best answers each question or best fits each statement and then fill in the corresponding circle on the answer sheet. A choice may be used once, more than once, or not at all in each set.

Questions 1–2 refer to the following parts of the cell cycle.

A) Anaphase

B) Prophase

C) Cytokinesis

D) Interphase

E) Metaphase

1

The point at which chromosomes are replicated to provide a full set of genetic material for both daughter cells

Choice (D) is the correct answer. In order to produce two daughter cells, the complete DNA must be replicated. This occurs during the S (synthesis) phase of interphase. During other stages of interphase, protein synthesis takes place and the centrioles replicate. Interphase is not technically part of mitosis.

2

The point at which the cytoplasm divides

Choice (C) is the correct answer. Cytokinesis is the process during which the cell actually divides in two. At this point, the two nuclei of the daughter cells are at opposite poles of the cell, and the cytoplasm separates. In animal cells, a contractile ring of cytoskeleton elements forms; the ring contracts and cleavage occurs to eventually form two daughter cells. In plant cells, a cell plate forms with new cell membranes for each cell. A new cell wall then forms between the two membranes of the cell plate.

Five-Choice Questions

The five-choice question is written either as an incomplete statement or as a question. It is appropriate when: (1) the problem presented is clearly delineated by the wording of the question so that you are asked to choose not a universal solution but the best of the solutions offered; (2) the problem is such that you are required to evaluate the relevance of five plausible, or even scientifically accurate, options and to select the one most pertinent; (3) the problem has several pertinent solutions and you are required to select the one inappropriate solution that is presented. Such questions normally contain a word in capital letters such as NOT, LEAST, or EXCEPT.

A special type of five-choice question is used in some tests, including the SAT Subject Test in Biology E/M, to allow for the possibility of multiple correct answers. For these questions, you must evaluate each response independently of the others in order to select the most appropriate combination. In questions of this type several (usually three or four) statements labeled by Roman numerals are given with the question. One or more of these statements may correctly answer the question. You must select from among the five lettered choices that follow the one combination of statements that best answers the question. In the test, questions of this type are mixed in with the more standard five-choice questions. (Question 5 is an example of this type of question.)

In five-choice questions, you may be asked to convert the information given in a word problem into graphical form or to select and apply the mathematical relationship necessary to solve the scientific problem. Alternatively, you may be asked to interpret experimental data, graphical stimulus, or mathematical expressions.

When the experimental data or other scientific problems to be analyzed are comparatively extensive, it is often convenient to organize several five-choice questions into sets, that is, to direct each question in a set to the same material. This practice allows you to answer several questions based on the same material. In no case, however, is the answer to one question necessary for answering a subsequent question correctly. Each question in a set is independent of the others but refers to the same material given for the entire set.

The following are directions for and examples of five-choice questions.

Directions: Each of the questions or incomplete statements below is followed by five suggested answers or completions. Some questions pertain to a set that refers to a laboratory or experimental situation. For each question, select the one choice that is the best answer to the question and then fill in the corresponding circle on the answer sheet.

Questions 3–4 refer to the following figure.

The figure below represents the percent germination of gourd seeds after being exposed to various treatments.

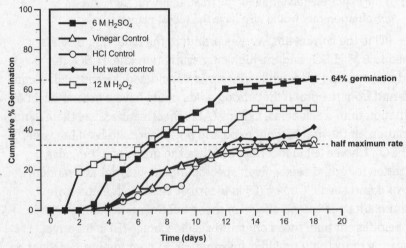

Cumulative germination of gourd seeds following various pregermination treatments.
n = 100 seeds per trial.

3

Which treatments reach more than a 30% germination rate by day 8?

A) 6 M H_2SO_4 only

B) 6 M H_2SO_4 and 12 M H_2O_2

C) Hot water control and vinegar control only

D) Vinegar control only

E) 6 M H_2SO_4, vinegar control and hot water control

Choice (B) is the correct answer. On day 8, the only treatments that have passed the 30% germination rate mark are 6 M H_2SO_4 and 12 M H_2O_2. Choice (A) is incorrect because it only includes the 6 M H_2SO_4 treatment. Choices (C), (D) and (E) are incorrect because they all include treatments that have not passed the 30% germination rate mark by day 8.

4

Which of the following can be inferred from the data?

A) Gourd seeds that are exposed to the hot water control would grow better if they were also exposed to 6 M H_2SO_4.

B) 64% is the highest possible germination rate for any group of gourd seeds.

C) Strong acids, like H_2SO_4, have a greater effect on germination than weak acids, like vinegar.

D) Tomato seeds would have similar responses to the same treatments.

E) If the experiment continued, the treatment with the highest germination rate would also have the tallest plants.

Choice (C) is the correct answer. According to the data, gourd seeds exposed to 6 M H_2SO_4 had the highest germination rate. H_2SO_4 is considered a strong acid, while vinegar is considered a weak acid. It can be inferred from the graph that strong acids could have a greater effect on germination than weak acids. Choice (A) is incorrect because there is no information on the graph about exposing gourd seeds to both hot water and H_2SO_4. Choice (B) is incorrect because the graph only provides information for gourd seeds given specific treatments, not any random group of gourd seeds. Choice (D) is incorrect because tomatoes are a different plant species; the effects of these treatments on tomato seeds could be different than those on gourd seeds. Choice (E) is incorrect because the graph only provides information on germination rates, not on the height of the gourd plants.

5

Meiosis is a type of cell division important in human gametogenesis (spermatogenesis and oogenesis). Which of the following statements about human gamete formation is correct?

A) The final step of gametogenesis results in the formation of two diploid cells.

B) The result of oogenesis is the formation of four fully functional ova.

C) Spermatogenesis and oogenesis are both regulated by a monthly cycle.

D) Oogenesis occurs throughout the lifetime of a female.

E) Spermatogenesis results in four fully functional sperm cells.

Choice (E) is the correct answer. In sperm production, all four products of meiosis become viable gametes. Choice (A) is incorrect because it describes the results of mitotic action, not meiosis, which results in twice as many nuclear products containing half the number of chromosomes (reduction division). Choice (B) is incorrect because oogenesis produces only one functional ova and three smaller polar bodies. Choice (C) is incorrect because spermatogenesis occurs continuously after puberty while ovulation and completion of oogenesis is regulated by a menstrual cycle. Choice (D) is incorrect because the actual production of viable eggs occurs only after puberty and ends after menopause.

6

In our current classification system, members that belong to the same order also belong to the same

A) genus
B) class
C) species
D) family
E) race

Choice (B) is the correct answer. In the Linnaean classification hierarchy, class is above order. Therefore, order members share the same class, phylum, and domain. Order members will not necessarily share the same genus, species name, or family, so choices (A), (C) and (D) are incorrect. Choice (E) is incorrect because race is a subdivision under species; it is defined as "a geographically isolated breeding population that shares certain characteristics in higher frequencies than other populations of that species, but has not become reproductively isolated."

7

The cells of the fruit fly *Drosophila melanogaster* contain 3 pairs of autosomal chromosomes and one pair of sex chromosomes. Upon completion of Meiosis II, how many chromosomes will each fruit fly gamete contain?

A) 2
B) 4
C) 6
D) 8
E) 16

Choice (B) is the correct answer. The process of meiosis is a reduction division that produces cells containing the haploid number of chromosomes. A fruit fly cell contains a total of 8 chromosomes arranged into 4 pairs. Replication will occur prior to meiosis, producing 16 chromosomes to be distributed. Upon completion of Meiosis II, four cells will be produced, and each cell will contain 4 chromosomes (half the original number and one from each of the 4 pairs).

8

Huntington's disease is a degenerative disorder of the nervous system that follows an inheritance pattern of autosomal dominance. What is the probability that a child will inherit Huntington's disease if one of the parents has an allele for the disease?

A) 0%

B) 25%

C) 50%

D) 75%

E) 100%

Choice (C) is the correct answer. Traits following a pattern of autosomal dominant inheritance do not need to be present in both alleles for expression to occur. If an individual inherits one copy of the Huntington's disease allele, he or she will have the disease. If one parent carries one allele for the disease, there is a 50% chance that the child will inherit the allele and have the disease.

9

Pattern baldness is a sex-linked recessive trait characterized by hair loss near the hairline and at the crown of the head. If a woman whose father is bald and a man who is bald have a son, what is the probability that the son will inherit the allele for pattern baldness? Assume that the woman's mother does not carry the allele for pattern baldness.

A) 0%

B) 25%

C) 50%

D) 75%

E) 100%

Choice (C) is the correct answer. Pattern baldness is a sex-linked recessive trait, which indicates that it is carried on the X-linked chromosome. A female inherits one X-linked chromosome from her father. Because the woman's mother does not carry the allele for pattern baldness, the woman only carries one copy of the allele. If the couple has a son, there is a 50% chance that the son will inherit the X-linked allele for pattern baldness from his mother. The father's baldness is irrelevant; he will pass his unaffected Y chromosome to the son.

10

Both avian and mammalian hearts are referred to as double-pump structures. Which of the following explains the anatomical and physiological basis for this description?

A) Blood always enters into an atrium and then is pumped into a ventricle.

B) Blood pressure alternates between systolic pressure and diastolic pressure.

C) The atria provide one pump and the ventricles provide a second pump.

D) The heart sends blood out through arteries and retrieves blood through veins.

E) The heart pumps blood simultaneously through a pulmonary circuit and a systemic circuit.

Choice (E) is the correct answer. The first pump sends oxygen-poor blood to the lungs and oxygen-rich blood back to the heart, which is pulmonary circulation. The second pump sends oxygen-rich blood to the rest of the body, which is systemic circulation. Choice (A) is incorrect because one atrium and one ventricle create a single pumping unit. Choice (B) is incorrect because systolic pressure and, together, diastolic pressure are simply measures of the pumping pressure in the systemic circulatory system. Choice (C) is incorrect because atria and ventricles work together to provide pumping pressure. The atria are receiving chambers and are too weak to work alone as pumps. Choice (D) is incorrect because arteries and veins are not pumping structures.

11

All of the following would be true of a population in Hardy-Weinberg equilibrium EXCEPT

A) There is no migration of individuals either into or out of the population.

B) The population is not influenced by selective pressures.

C) Mating occurs randomly within the population.

D) There is no change in the rate of mutation.

E) The population is relatively small.

Choice (E) is the correct answer. The Hardy-Weinberg equilibrium is used to determine the shift in allele frequency within a population. The introduction or loss of genes will have a greater effect on a small population than it would on a large population. Choices (A), (B), (C) and (D) are incorrect because they are all requirements for Hardy-Weinberg equilibrium (no occurrence of evolution). The Hardy-Weinberg equilibrium predicts gene flow patterns within a population and assumes alleles will be inherited in similar ratios to those of the parents over several generations. This genetic equilibrium is maintained if few new genes are introduced to the population.

12

There is a high degree of homology in the DNA of dogs and wolves. Which of the following best explains why dogs and wolves show a high degree of similarity in their DNA?

A) Dogs and wolves have the same number of chromosomes.

B) The morphologies of dogs and wolves are similar.

C) Dogs and wolves share the same ecological niche.

D) Dogs and wolves share a very recent common ancestor.

E) The high degree of homology is the result of convergent evolution.

Choice (D) is the correct answer. Homology refers to traits that two different organisms inherit from a common ancestor. The best explanation for the high degree of homology in the DNA of dogs and wolves is that dogs and wolves share a very recent common ancestor. Choice (A) is incorrect. Although it is true that dogs and wolves both have 78 chromosomes, chromosome number does not necessarily indicate a close relationship (for example, chickens also have 78 chromosomes). Choice (B) refers only to morphology, which describes the form and structure of an organism but does not discuss its inherited traits; two organisms can share certain morphological features but may not be genetically related. Choice (C) describes the relative position of species within a habitat where organisms live, which does not affect DNA. Choice (E) describes convergent evolution, which means that a similar characteristic evolved within two separate lineages independently, usually due to similar environmental challenges. Since dogs and wolves share a high degree of homology in their DNA, their similarities are genetically based, and not independent of one another.

13

Darwin based his ideas of natural selection based on all of the following observations EXCEPT

A) Parents pass their successful traits on to their offspring.

B) Population members exhibit variations in many traits.

C) All living organisms use the same genetic code.

D) Environmental pressures can select various traits based on survivability.

E) Populations that adapt to environmental conditions produce many offspring.

Choice (C) is the correct answer. The structure of DNA was not discovered until the 1950s; Darwin could not possibly have had knowledge of the genetic code. Choices (A), (B), (D) and (E) are incorrect because they do support Darwin's theory of evolution. Darwin conducted direct observations of various species and he noted that parents with the most favorable traits survive to have offspring who receive those favorable traits; that there is variety in traits; that there is relative success or failure based on environmental conditions; and that species seem to overpopulate.

14

Which of the following is LEAST likely to result in speciation?

A) Random mating among members of a large population of a species

B) Occurrence of hybridization between individuals from two different species

C) Development of different mating behavior by some members of a species

D) Emigration to a specialized microenvironment by some members of a species

E) Formation of a physical barrier that blocks gene flow between members of a species

Choice (A) is the correct answer. Random mating is considered to be one of the factors that maintains gene flow within a species and therefore should show no change with time, or evolution of the species. Choice (B) is incorrect because hybridization can be a factor in speciation, especially in some plant species. Choice (C) is incorrect because differences in mating behavior that prevent successful mating are considered reproductive isolating mechanisms and can lead to speciation. Choices (D) and (E) are incorrect because both emigration and the formation of physical barriers lead to isolation of a subpopulation, which can lead to genetic divergence of the subpopulation from the original population, which can lead to speciation.

E Section (Ecological)

Directions: Each of the questions or incomplete statements below is followed by five suggested answers or completions. Some questions pertain to a set that refers to a laboratory or experimental situation. For each question, select the one choice that is the best answer to the question and then fill in the corresponding circle on the answer sheet.

15

Which of the following is the best predictor of high population growth rates within specific countries?

A) Carrying capacity

B) Increase in agricultural technology

C) Declining birth rates in developed countries

D) Improved nutrition across the globe

E) Age structure

Choice (E) is the correct answer. Age structure is the percentage of the population at each age within a country. Often depicted graphically, an age structure diagram can predict a population's growth trends and indicate future social structures. A uniform distribution across age groups indicates stable population size. A population that has a much higher distribution among young people will show rapid population growth. A population with a higher distribution among elderly people will show a decline in population growth. Choice (A) is incorrect because carrying capacity, the maximum population a particular environment can support, cannot be used to predict population growth rates in different countries. Although an increase in agricultural technology could affect a population's ability to grow, choice (B) is incorrect because it is not the best factor to determine population growth rates in specific countries. Choice (C) is incorrect because information about population growth rates in *developed* countries would not help in determining high population growth rates in developing countries. Although improved nutrition across the globe can affect population growth, choice (D) is incorrect because it is not the best factor to determine population growth rates in specific countries.

16

Which of the following nutrient cycles has its largest reservoir in the atmosphere?

A) Carbon cycle

B) Nitrogen cycle

C) Potassium cycle

D) Phosphorus cycle

E) Water cycle

Choice (B) is the correct answer. Nitrogen makes up 80% of the atmosphere. It is incorporated into the biosphere via work by microorganisms that can break the triple covalent bonds of N_2 and fix it into NH_3 and, later, into nitrites and nitrates that are taken up by plants for use in biosyntheses. Choice (A) is incorrect because CO_2 is only 0.04% of the atmosphere; most carbon is reservoired in sediments and rocks. Choices (C) and (D) are incorrect because potassium and phosphorus are rarely in gaseous form. Choice (E) is incorrect because atmospheric water is the smallest source of H_2O, with oceans serving as the major reservoir for water.

17

A shrubland was studied to determine its metabolic rate. The data from the study show that the energy being released by respiration was less than the energy captured during photosynthesis. What phenomenon is taking place in this terrestrial plant community?

A) Major plant species are dying.

B) Biomass of the community is increasing.

C) Biomass of the community is decreasing.

D) The rate of plant reproduction is increasing.

E) A secondary succession of plants is growing in an established community.

Choice (B) is the correct answer. This question refers to net primary productivity. An ecosystem's net primary production is measured by the amount of light energy converted to chemical energy by autotrophs minus the energy those organisms must use to survive. In other words, it is the amount of new "food" or biomass available to consumers. If more energy were captured during photosynthesis than was released by respiration, the biomass must be increasing. Choice (A) is incorrect because the data describe an increase in primary productivity, so major plant species probably are not dying. Choice (C) is incorrect because a decrease in the biomass of the community would mean that the energy being released by respiration was more than the energy captured during photosynthesis, which is the opposite of what the question is asking. Choice (D) is incorrect because multiplication of producers is irrelevant; it is the efficiency of the producers present that will determine productivity. Choice (E) is incorrect because the question refers to the amount of energy, not the type of plant species present in the community.

18

A food chain consists of producers, primary consumers, secondary consumers and tertiary consumers. If the producers produce 1000 kcal of energy, how many kcal are theoretically available to the secondary consumers based on normal trophic efficiencies?

A) 1000

B) 100

C) 10

D) 1

E) 0.5

Choice (C) is the correct answer. 10 kcal of energy are available to the secondary consumers. As energy flows through a food chain, it is incorporated by the organisms at each level. Although some energy will be utilized for cellular metabolism, most of it is lost as heat. As a result, approximately 10% is available for transfer to the next trophic level (known as the 10% rule). If the producers produce 1000 kcal of energy, then 100 kcal will be available to the primary consumers, 10 kcal will be available to the secondary consumers, and 1 kcal will be available to the tertiary consumers.

19

A sample of living tissue of a fish-eating bird species was found to have a concentration of a specific heavy metal of 700,000 ppt (parts per trillion). What is the best inferential explanation you could make based on these data?

A) Air pollution may have caused this bird species to inhale dangerous amounts of heavy metals while migrating.

B) The entire population of the bird species, from which this sample was taken, died.

C) The population of this bird species exploded, causing an ecosystem imbalance.

D) Pollutants tend to collect in areas of land where this bird species nests.

E) This bird species is at a high trophic level on the food chain.

Choice (E) is the correct answer. This question deals with biomagnification. Organisms at higher trophic levels in a food chain can experience biomagnification, which is the accumulation of environmental toxins (such as heavy metals) in living tissue. Organisms at lower trophic levels accumulate small amounts of toxins through their food. Because organisms at the next highest trophic level eat many of the lower-level organisms, they take in higher amounts of the toxins. At the highest trophic levels, increased concentrations of toxins in organisms' tissues can be dangerous. This bird tissue has a high concentration of a specific heavy metal, so the species must be at a high trophic level. Choice (A) is incorrect because even though there can be heavy metals in air pollution, the major cause of heavy metals in the tissue of fish-eating birds is biomagnification. Choice (B) is incorrect because the high concentration of heavy metal in the tissue of one fish-eating bird does not imply that all birds of that species in the population died. Choice (C) is incorrect because a high concentration of heavy metals is not in any way related to the explosive increase of populations; in fact, it can have the opposite effect. Choice (D) is incorrect because land pollutants would be in the soil. This species eats fish rather than soil organisms or plants, so the heavy metals present in a toxic soil wouldn't make their way into the bird's tissue at such high levels.

M Section (Molecular)

Directions: Each of the questions or incomplete statements below is followed by five suggested answers or completions. Some questions pertain to a set that refers to a laboratory or experimental situation. For each question, select the one choice that is the best answer to the question and then fill in the corresponding circle on the answer sheet.

20

Which of the following statements regarding mitosis is correct?

A) Mitosis will result in reduction division.

B) Sister chromatids will separate during metaphase.

C) Cytokinesis occurs during the process of prophase.

D) Mitosis occurs continually in the life cycle of all somatic cells.

E) The final product of mitosis is the formation of two identical nuclei.

Choice (E) is the correct answer. Mitosis is a process that produces two diploid nuclei that are genetically identical to the original. Choice (A) is incorrect because meiosis, not mitosis, reduces the final chromosome number by half. Choice (B) is incorrect because sister chromatids separate during anaphase. Choice (C) is incorrect because cytokinesis occurs at the end of telophase, not during prophase. Choice (D) is incorrect because some somatic cells, such as certain neurons and skeletal muscle cells, do not divide once they are fully differentiated.

21

The process of photosynthesis occurs in two steps. One step is referred to as the light-dependent reactions, and the other is the light-independent reactions. Which of the following events occurs during the light-independent reactions?

A) The production of oxygen

B) The splitting of a molecule of water

C) The production of ATP

D) The production of G3P

E) The formation of NADPH

Choice (D) is the correct answer. The production of G3P occurs in the stroma of the chloroplast, using products of the light reactions (ATP and NADPH) to fix carbon in either light or dark conditions. Choices (A), (B), (C) and (E) all occur during the light-dependent reactions and are necessary for the capture and conversion of energy. Only choice (D), the production of G3P, is an event that does not directly require light.

22

Changes in temperature and pH often have great effects on the efficiency of enzymes because

A) the energy of activation will be raised or lowered.

B) the three-dimensional protein structure of enzymes is altered.

C) changes affect substrate surfaces and make them unrecognizable.

D) all enzymes work best at normal body temperature and a neutral pH.

E) cofactors are not available under abnormal conditions.

Choice (B) is the correct answer. Both temperature and pH can alter tertiary protein structure, changing the active site where enzymatic activity occurs. There is a certain optimal temperature at which an enzyme's catalytic activity is greatest. Above this temperature, the enzyme structure denatures because intra- and intermolecular bonds are broken. Each enzyme also works within a specific pH range. Changes in pH can make and break intra- and intermolecular bonds. Choice (A) is incorrect because the energy of activation does not change. Choice (C) is incorrect because it does not address the effect on the enzyme. Choice (D) is incorrect because enzymes have different optimal conditions depending on their location in the body and function. Choice (E) is incorrect because cofactor availability would not normally be affected by physical conditions.

Biology E/M Subject Test - Practice Test 1

Practice Helps

The test that follows is an actual, previously administered SAT Subject Test in Biology E/M. To get an idea of what it's like to take this test, practice under conditions that are much like those of an actual test administration.

- Set aside an hour when you can take the test uninterrupted.

- Sit at a desk or table with no other books or papers. Dictionaries, other books, or notes are not allowed in the test room.

- Tear out an answer sheet from the back of this book and fill it in just as you would on the day of the test. One answer sheet can be used for up to three Subject Tests.

- Read the instructions that precede the practice test. During the actual administration you will be asked to read them before answering test questions.

- Time yourself by placing a clock or kitchen timer in front of you.

- After you finish the practice test, read the sections "How to Score the SAT Subject Test in Ecological Biology" or "How to Score the SAT Subject Test in Molecular Biology" and "How Did You Do on the Subject Test in Ecological Biology?" or "How Did You Do on the Subject Test in Molecular Biology?"

- The appearance of the answer sheet in this book may differ from the answer sheet you see on test day.

BIOLOGY–E TEST or BIOLOGY–M TEST

You must decide whether you want to take a Biology Test with Ecological Emphasis (BIOLOGY-E) or Molecular Emphasis (BIOLOGY-M) now, before the test begins. The top portion of the page of the answer sheet that you will use to take the Biology Test you have selected must be filled in exactly as illustrated below. When your supervisor tells you to fill in the circle next to the name of the test you are about to take, mark your answer sheet as shown.

For BIOLOGY-E

○ Literature	○ Mathematics Level 1	○ German	○ Chinese Listening	○ Japanese Listening
● Biology E	○ Mathematics Level 2	○ Italian	○ French Listening	○ Korean Listening
○ Biology M	○ U.S. History	○ Latin	○ German Listening	○ Spanish Listening
○ Chemistry	○ World History	○ Modern Hebrew		
○ Physics	○ French	○ Spanish	Background Questions: ① ② ③ ④ ⑤ ⑥ ⑦ ⑧ ⑨

For BIOLOGY-M

○ Literature	○ Mathematics Level 1	○ German	○ Chinese Listening	○ Japanese Listening
○ Biology E	○ Mathematics Level 2	○ Italian	○ French Listening	○ Korean Listening
● Biology M	○ U.S. History	○ Latin	○ German Listening	○ Spanish Listening
○ Chemistry	○ World History	○ Modern Hebrew		
○ Physics	○ French	○ Spanish	Background Questions: ① ② ③ ④ ⑤ ⑥ ⑦ ⑧ ⑨

After filling in the circle next to the name of the test you are taking, locate the Background Questions section, which also appears at the top of your answer sheet (as shown above). This is where you will answer the following Background Questions on your answer sheet.

BACKGROUND QUESTIONS

Please answer the four questions below by filling in the appropriate circle in the Background Questions box on your answer sheet. The information you provide is for statistical purposes only and will not affect your test score.

Question I   How many semesters of biology have you taken in high school? (If you are taking biology this semester, count it as a full semester.) Fill in only one circle of circles 1-3.

- One semester or less   — Fill in circle 1.
- Two semesters   — Fill in circle 2.
- Three semesters or more   — Fill in circle 3.

Question II   Which of the following best describes your biology course? Fill in only one circle of circles 4-6.

- General Biology   — Fill in circle 4.
- Biology with emphasis on ecology   — Fill in circle 5.
- Biology with emphasis on molecular biology — Fill in circle 6.

Question III Which of the following best describes your background in algebra? (If you are taking an algebra course this semester, count it as a full semester.) Fill in only one circle of circles 7-8.

- One semester or less   — Fill in circle 7.
- Two semesters or more   — Fill in circle 8.

Question IV   Have you had or are you currently taking Advanced Placement Biology? If you are, fill in circle 9.

When the supervisor gives the signal, turn the page and begin the Biology Test. There are 100 numbered circles on the answer sheet. There are 60 questions in the core Biology Test, 20 questions in the Biology-E section, and 20 questions in the Biology-M section. Therefore use ONLY circles 1-80 (for Biology-E) OR circles 1-60 plus 81-100 (for Biology-M) for recording your answers.

BIOLOGY-E/M TEST

FOR BOTH BIOLOGY-E AND BIOLOGY-M,
ANSWER QUESTIONS 1-60

Directions: Each set of lettered choices below refers to the numbered questions or statements immediately following it. Select the one lettered choice that best answers each question or best fits each statement and then fill in the corresponding circle on the answer sheet. A choice may be used once, more than once, or not at all in each set.

Questions 1-4 refer to the following.

(A) Characteristic of plants but not animals
(B) Characteristic of animals but not plants
(C) Characteristic of eukaryotes but not prokaryotes
(D) Characteristic of prokaryotes but not eukaryotes
(E) Characteristic of all organisms

1. The cells of an organism contain mitochondria.

2. The cells of an organism contain ribosomes.

3. The cell wall is composed of cellulose.

4. The cytosol of an organism's cells is contained by the plasma membrane.

Questions 5-7 refer to the following mammalian structures.

(A) Oviduct
(B) Uterus
(C) Ovary
(D) Epididymis
(E) Testes

5. Site of implantation of the blastocyst

6. Site of gametogenesis from puberty until death

7. Site of fertilization

Questions 8-10 refer to the following conditions of Hardy-Weinberg equilibrium.

(A) Very large population size
(B) No migration
(C) No net mutation
(D) Random mating
(E) No natural selection

8. The condition that is not met if individuals choose mates based on a phenotypic trait

9. The condition that is not met when a new nucleotide sequence appears in the gene pool

10. The condition that is not met if there is differential survival of one of the genotypes in the population

GO ON TO THE NEXT PAGE

Questions 11-14 refer to the following.

Islands *A*, *B*, *C*, *D*, and *E* are recently formed volcanic islands. They will all develop different levels of biodiversity. Assume that the species populating the five islands will all come from the mainland.

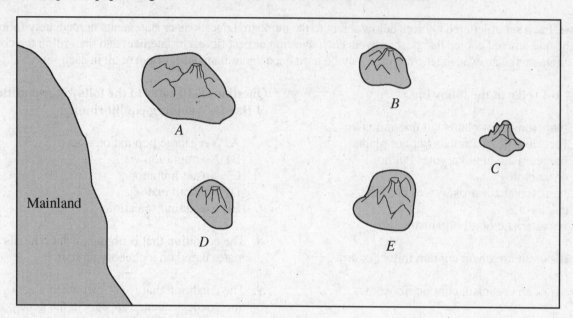

11. Island expected to have the greatest biodiversity

12. Island expected to have the lowest immigration rate of new species

13. Island expected to have the lowest extinction rate

14. Island expected to have the lowest biodiversity

GO ON TO THE NEXT PAGE

Directions: Each of the questions or incomplete statements below is followed by five suggested answers or completions. Some questions pertain to a set that refers to a laboratory or experimental situation. For each question, select the one choice that is the best answer to the question and then fill in the corresponding circle on the answer sheet.

15. The pH of human blood is closest to

    (A) 3.5
    (B) 5.5
    (C) 7.5
    (D) 9.5
    (E) 10.5

16. A geneticist wishes to determine whether a black guinea pig carries the recessive gene for white fur. Which of the following would best reveal the possible presence of the masked recessive trait?

    (A) Examining the undersurface of the guinea pig for white hairs dispersed among the black
    (B) Studying one of the guinea pig's hair follicles with an electron microscope
    (C) Analyzing the skin cells of the guinea pig chemically for the nature of its messenger RNA
    (D) Examining the bands in the guinea pig's salivary gland chromosomes
    (E) Mating the black guinea pig with a white one and observing whether any of the offspring are white

17. Which of the following can increase genetic variability by the exchange of segments between homologous chromosomes?

    (A) Point mutation
    (B) Linkage
    (C) Polyploidy
    (D) Nondisjunction
    (E) Crossing-over

18. Which of the following statements about thermoregulation is true?

    (A) Endotherms maintain body temperature with metabolic heat.
    (B) Endotherm body temperature is always greater than ambient temperature.
    (C) Endotherms always have much higher blood temperature than do ectotherms.
    (D) Ectotherms do not have a method to maintain body temperature.
    (E) Ectotherms can perform vigorous activity for longer periods of time than can endotherms.

19. The flowering plant *Mirabilis jalapa* produces flowers that may be red, white, or pink. When red-flowered plants are crossed with white-flowered plants, all offspring have pink flowers. In an experiment, pink-flowered plants were crossed with each other. Of the 200 offspring produced, approximately 50 had red flowers, 50 had white flowers, and 100 had pink flowers. The most likely inheritance pattern for flower color in the plant is

    (A) polygenic inheritance
    (B) complete dominance
    (C) multiple alleles
    (D) incomplete dominance
    (E) sex-linkage

GO ON TO THE NEXT PAGE

	G	*g*
G	*GG*	*Gg*
g	*Gg*	*gg*

20. In the cross represented in the Punnett square above, *G* is the allele for green, and *g* is the allele for yellow. Assuming a large number of offspring, the Punnett square predicts that

(A) 25% of the offspring will be yellow
(B) 25% of the offspring will not survive
(C) 50% of the offspring will be homozygous yellow
(D) 50% of the offspring will be homozygous green
(E) 75% of the offspring will be heterozygous green

21. A chemical compound formed by combining <u>one</u> adenine molecule, <u>one</u> ribose molecule, and <u>one</u> phosphate group is

(A) an amino acid
(B) a nucleotide
(C) ATP
(D) RNA
(E) DNA

22. Bacteria play an important role in the fixation of nitrogen by converting atmospheric nitrogen into

(A) DNA
(B) oxygen
(C) ammonia
(D) a hydrocarbon
(E) an amino acid

23. Characteristics found in fungi include all of the following EXCEPT

(A) asexual reproduction
(B) cell walls composed of chitin
(C) presence of membrane-bound organelles
(D) production of spores
(E) production of seed-containing fruit

24. A symbiotic relationship between two species that is beneficial to both is defined as

(A) mutualism
(B) commensalism
(C) neutralism
(D) parasitism
(E) predation

25. Which of the following is always required for successful sexual reproduction in multicellular plants or animals?

(A) Nonmotile eggs and sperm
(B) Gametes that are haploid
(C) A zygote produced by mitosis
(D) Two pairs of chromosomes per gamete
(E) Two pairs of centrioles

26. Which of the following is an accurate statement about endosperm and yolk?

(A) Both provide stored energy for the embryo.
(B) Both are found in flowering plants.
(C) Both contain triploid cells.
(D) Both contain toxins or bitter compounds for protection from animal predation.
(E) Both are produced by the male parent.

27. Which of the following organisms appeared earliest on Earth?

(A) Ferns
(B) Mosses
(C) Fungi
(D) Bacteria
(E) Lichens

28. Which of the following represents the normal path of blood flow in mammals?

(A) Lungs, right atrium, left atrium, right ventricle, left ventricle, aorta
(B) Right atrium, lungs, left atrium, right ventricle, left ventricle, aorta
(C) Right atrium, lungs, left atrium, left ventricle, right ventricle, aorta
(D) Right atrium, right ventricle, lungs, left atrium, left ventricle, aorta
(E) Left atrium, left ventricle, lungs, right atrium, right ventricle, aorta

GO ON TO THE NEXT PAGE

29. Which of the following is the property of CO_2 that leads scientists to link increasing CO_2 levels with global warming?

(A) CO_2 is a relatively dense gas, and higher levels cause the atmosphere to thin and distribute more of the equatorial heat to higher latitudes.

(B) CO_2 is one of the greenhouse gases, and higher levels keep some heat trapped in Earth's atmosphere.

(C) CO_2 molecules react chemically with gases in the ozone layer, thereby destroying the ability of these gases to block most of the Sun's harmful radiation.

(D) CO_2 is the product of combustion and results primarily from forest fires that have heated Earth's atmosphere.

(E) CO_2 transmits radiation, and increased CO_2 in the upper atmosphere will enable more short-wave radiation to reach Earth's surface.

30. A man in his early twenties learns that his father has been diagnosed with Huntington's disease. This rare disease is caused by a dominant allele and usually does not manifest itself until middle age. There is no history of the disease in the young man's mother's family. What is the probability that the young man will develop the symptoms of the disease when he is older?

(A) 0%
(B) 25%
(C) 50%
(D) 66%
(E) 75%

31. Which of the following hormones regulates water conservation in the human body?

(A) Follicle-stimulating hormone (FSH)
(B) Insulin
(C) Prolactin
(D) Antidiuretic hormone (ADH)
(E) Oxytocin

32. Which of the following would be LEAST useful in constructing a phylogenetic tree of the mammals?

(A) The fossil record
(B) Nucleotide sequences
(C) Amino acid sequences
(D) Tooth structure
(E) Dietary requirements

33. A factor associated with the opening of stomata is the movement of potassium ions into the guard cells. How do entering potassium ions affect guard cells?

(A) They promote the movement of water into the cells by osmosis.
(B) They cause the guard cells to shrink, opening the stomata.
(C) They maintain the osmotic integrity of the cells.
(D) They disrupt the normal function of the plasma membranes.
(E) They activate water channels in the plasma membranes.

34. Which of the following is the best description of lymph?

(A) Lymph consists of red and white blood cells, platelets, and plasma contained in lymph vessels.
(B) Lymph consists of erythrocytes that have leaked out of blood vessels and bathe body cells.
(C) Lymph contains antihistamines that are important in fighting bacterial infections.
(D) Lymph consists of interstitial fluid re-collected into lymph vessels from the spaces between body cells.
(E) Lymph is produced at specific sites called lymph nodes.

GO ON TO THE NEXT PAGE

35. In the illustrations below, animals with one opening to the digestive tract and two layers of tissues include which of the following?

I.
II.
III.
IV.

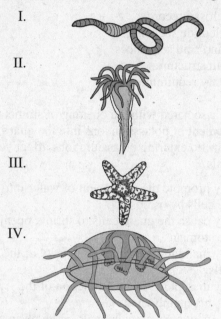

(A) I only
(B) II only
(C) III only
(D) II and IV
(E) III and IV

36. A tree stands 6 meters high and is 0.20 meter in diameter. A branch falls leaving a scar that is 0.90 meter above the ground. In 20 years if the tree is 36 meters high, that scar will be how far from the ground?

(A) 18.00 meters
(B) 12.00 meters
(C) 7.20 meters
(D) 6.00 meters
(E) 0.90 meter

37. Which of the following best describes different alleles of a single gene?

(A) They exhibit an identical nucleotide base sequence.
(B) They may code for related proteins affecting the same trait.
(C) They code for unrelated proteins at different sites on the same chromosome.
(D) They occupy different positions on the same chromosome.
(E) They are found on complementary strands of the same DNA molecule.

38. The most dangerous aspect of the use of the pesticide DDT is that it

(A) kills plants as well as insects
(B) accumulates in higher trophic levels
(C) leaches nitrogen from the soil
(D) depletes the ozone layer
(E) can be used as food by harmful bacteria

39. At the boundary between two major layers of rock in Earth's surface—the Cretaceous and Tertiary—geologists have found a thin layer of rock enriched in iridium, an element that is very rare on Earth. This is part of the evidence suggesting that dinosaurs became extinct because of

(A) the impact of a meteor
(B) brain function that was inferior to mammals'
(C) a climate change that brought freezing temperatures to the Northern Hemisphere
(D) extensive flooding from melting ice caps
(E) a disease epidemic caused by unusual microorganisms

GO ON TO THE NEXT PAGE

40. Which of the following adaptations in vertebrates enabled them to colonize early terrestrial environments successfully?

  (A) Lungs, efficient kidneys, amniotic eggs
  (B) Ovaries and testes, wings, four-chambered heart
  (C) Backbone, teeth, waterproof skin
  (D) Binocular vision, closed circulatory system, lungs
  (E) Efficient kidneys, four-chambered heart, scales

41. In humans, color-blindness is a recessive, sex-linked trait. A woman with normal color vision, whose father was color-blind, marries a man with normal color vision. What percentage of their sons will probably be color-blind?

  (A)   0%
  (B) 25%
  (C) 50%
  (D) 75%
  (E) 100%

42. What would most likely occur if an organism is homozygous for an allele that encodes a defective digestive enzyme?

  (A) More enzyme molecules would be produced to compensate.
  (B) Another gene would synthesize the normal, functional enzyme.
  (C) The organism's homeostasis would be compromised.
  (D) The organism would be more susceptible to mutations.
  (E) The evolution of the organism with this defect would progress at a faster rate.

GO ON TO THE NEXT PAGE

Questions 43-45

The results of an experiment comparing the effects of four antibiotics on the growth of a strain of bacteria are shown below. The bacteria were grown on nutrient agar. The amount of antibiotic is the same on each paper disk. The diagram shows the results after one day. The areas of no growth are white.

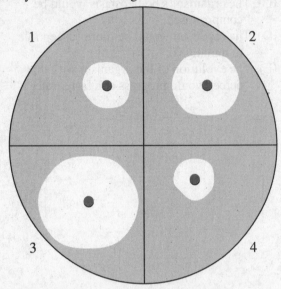

Quadrant 1 - Paper disk with Streptomycin
Quadrant 2 - Paper disk with Erythromycin
Quadrant 3 - Paper disk with Tetracycline
Quadrant 4 - Paper disk with Penicillin

43. Based on the results of the experiment, the best treatment to eliminate an infection with this strain of bacteria would be

(A) penicillin
(B) tetracycline
(C) streptomycin only
(D) erythromycin only
(E) erythromycin and streptomycin

44. The plate was examined the following day and small colonies were observed within the white area of the penicillin treatment. Which of the following is the best explanation for this new growth?

(A) This strain of bacteria grows well on all types of media.
(B) Penicillin is an ineffective antibiotic.
(C) Penicillin resistance is present in all bacterial strains.
(D) This strain of bacteria contained plasmids that promote growth in the presence of all antibiotics.
(E) The new colonies represent bacteria with penicillin resistance.

45. Which of the following in a petri dish would be the most appropriate control for this experiment?

(A) No antibiotics, no bacteria, and no agar
(B) A mixture of other antibiotics on paper disks on nutrient agar
(C) Antibiotics, but no bacteria on different nutrient agar
(D) Bacteria and a paper disk with no antibiotic on the same plate
(E) Bacteria placed in the dark on the same nutrient agar

GO ON TO THE NEXT PAGE

Questions 46-49

The following is a sequence of nucleotides found in a human gene.

I. TAG TAG AAA CCA CAA AGG ATA

Individuals with a certain genetic condition have the following sequence at the same position.

II. TAG TAG CCA CAA AGG ATA

46. The letters A, T, G, and C represent

(A) nucleotides
(B) amino acids
(C) proteins
(D) monosaccharides
(E) phosphates

47. The condition occurs only when a person has two copies of sequence II, which indicates that the allele for the condition is

(A) dominant
(B) recessive
(C) sex-linked
(D) codominant
(E) heterozygous

48. Which of the following is true about the difference in gene products of sequences I and II ?

(A) Sequence II will produce a protein with the same primary structure as a protein produced by sequence I.
(B) Sequence II will produce a protein that is one amino acid longer than a protein produced by sequence I.
(C) Sequence II will produce a protein with several different amino acids than a protein produced by sequence I.
(D) Sequence II will produce a protein that is much longer than a protein produced by sequence I.
(E) Sequence II will produce a protein that is one amino acid shorter than a protein produced by sequence I.

49. The mutation that led to the difference between sequence I and sequence II is best described as which of the following?

(A) Frameshift
(B) Substitution
(C) Inversion
(D) Translocation
(E) Deletion

GO ON TO THE NEXT PAGE

Questions 50-53

In an experiment, five groups of germinating corn seeds were studied to determine the effects of pH on growth. Each group of ten corn seeds was germinated in a petri dish containing a paper towel moistened with an equal amount of an aqueous solution at a specific pH. All petri dishes were exposed to the same light and temperature conditions. After five days of germination, the radicles (embryonic roots) of all seeds in a pH group were measured. The table shows the results from the experiment.

THE EFFECTS OF VARYING pH ON THE GERMINATION OF CORN SEEDS

Group Number	pH Used	Average Radicle Length (cm)
1	4	3
2	6	4.6
3	7	5.7
4	8	3.6
5	10	2.8

50. From the data, the optimal pH for the radicle growth of germinated corn seeds is most likely

    (A) pH 4

    (B) pH 6

    (C) pH 7

    (D) pH 8

    (E) pH 10

51. Which of the following is the independent (manipulated) variable in the experiment?

    (A) The number of days for germination
    (B) The number of corn seeds used
    (C) The growth of the radicles
    (D) The pH used
    (E) The temperature used

52. All of the following statements about radicle growth in the corn seeds are true EXCEPT:

    (A) Starch was digested in the seed to provide energy for growth.
    (B) Uptake of water initiated the germination process.
    (C) The temperature used was adequate for enzyme activity to occur in the seeds.
    (D) The corn seeds have proven to be metabolically active.
    (E) Low levels of light directly provided the energy needed for germination.

53. Which of the following conditions is (are) controlled in the experiment?

    I. Light
    II. Temperature
    III. pH used

    (A) I only
    (B) II only
    (C) III only
    (D) I and II only
    (E) I, II, and III

GO ON TO THE NEXT PAGE

Questions 54-57

The diagram below shows a terminal (end) portion of the nervous system of a segmented earthworm. The cell bodies of the neurons are arranged in groups, each of which is called a ganglion.

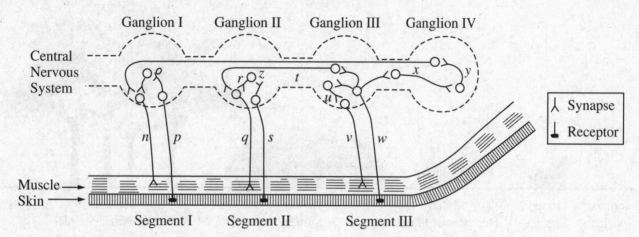

54. What effect would the destruction of neuron *n* have on the earthworm?

   (A) The skin at segment I would not receive stimuli.
   (B) The muscular movements at only segment I would be stopped.
   (C) The muscular movements at segment II as well as those at segment I would be stopped.
   (D) Neuron *p* would deteriorate.
   (E) Neuron *z* would deteriorate.

55. If the worm is touched at segment III, the muscles in that segment contract. Which of the following are the only neurons that must be involved in this stimulus-response action?

   (A) *q, r, s*
   (B) *q, t, w*
   (C) *w, u, v*
   (D) *n, z, y, x, w*
   (E) *s, r, t, u, v*

56. If the worm is touched at segment III and the muscles in segment II respond, which of the following neurons must be involved in the segment II response?

   (A) *s, r, q*
   (B) *s, t, v*
   (C) *w, u, v*
   (D) *w, t, q*
   (E) *q, t, u, v*

57. If neuron *y* in ganglion IV were destroyed, which of the following would be the result?

   (A) Segment I could not respond to a stimulus at the skin of segment I.
   (B) Segment I could not respond to a stimulus at the skin of segment III.
   (C) Segment II could not respond to a stimulus at the skin of segment II.
   (D) Segment II could not respond to a stimulus at the skin of segment III.
   (E) Segment III could not respond to a stimulus at the skin of segment III.

GO ON TO THE NEXT PAGE

Questions 58-60

Succession from bare rock to mature forest in a terrestrial ecosystem is diagrammed below.

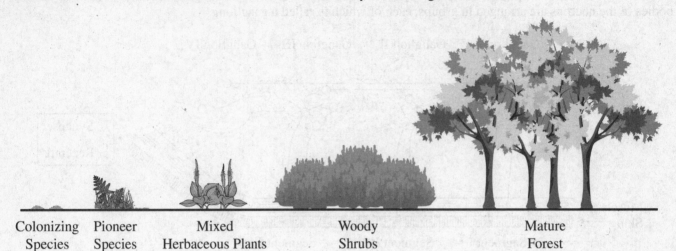

| Colonizing Species | Pioneer Species | Mixed Herbaceous Plants | Woody Shrubs | Mature Forest |

58. Which of the following organisms are most likely to be the first colonizing species?

(A) Mushrooms
(B) Lichens
(C) Grasses
(D) Slime molds
(E) Phytoplankton

59. Which of the following is the most logical explanation for why the colonizing species preceded the pioneer species in the ecological succession?

(A) When the colonizers first inhabited the ecosystem, there was not enough sunlight to support the pioneer species.
(B) The soils were initially too acidic for the pioneer species.
(C) The colonizing species secreted chemicals that inhibited the growth of pioneer species.
(D) The colonizing species made the habitat more suitable for the pioneer species.
(E) The colonizing species had to accumulate enough mutations to become pioneer species.

60. The terrestrial ecosystem most likely belongs in which of the following biomes?

(A) Tundra
(B) Taiga (coniferous forest)
(C) Temperate deciduous forest
(D) Chaparral
(E) Desert

If you are taking the Biology-E test, continue with questions 61-80.
If you are taking the Biology-M test, go to question 81 now.

GO ON TO THE NEXT PAGE ▶

Directions: Each set of lettered choices below refers to the numbered questions or statements immediately following it. Select the one lettered choice that best answers each question or best fits each statement and then fill in the corresponding circle on the answer sheet. A choice may be used once, more than once, or not at all in each set.

Questions 61-62

The figure below represents proposed relationships among the animal phyla. Selected nodes are labeled.

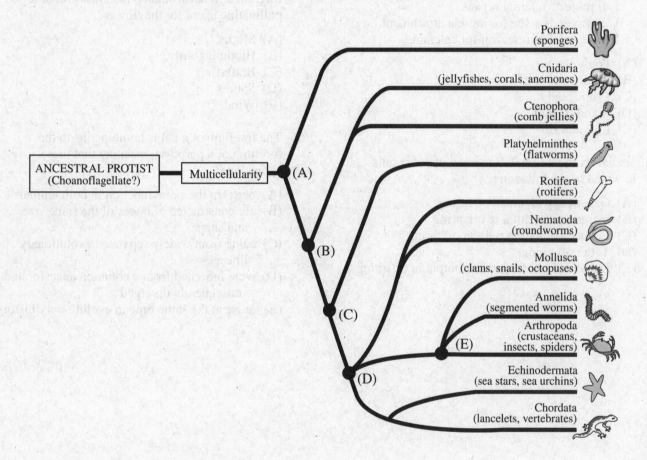

61. Node that represents separation of those animals with no true tissues from all others

62. Node where protostomes are separated from deuterostomes

GO ON TO THE NEXT PAGE

Directions: Each of the questions or incomplete statements below is followed by five suggested answers or completions. Some questions pertain to a set that refers to a laboratory or experimental situation. For each question, select the one choice that is the best answer to the question and then fill in the corresponding circle on the answer sheet.

63. In vertebrates, the bony endoskeleton performs which of the following functions?

    I. It protects internal organs.
   II. It serves as a site for muscle attachment.
  III. It serves as a reservoir for calcium.

(A) I only
(B) II only
(C) I and II only
(D) II and III only
(E) I, II, and III

64. Sexual reproduction in flowering plants results in which of the following?

(A) Genetically identical offspring
(B) Increased variation in offspring
(C) Reduced mutation rates in offspring
(D) Taller offspring
(E) Decreased photosynthetic output in offspring

65. A particular species of flower blooms at night with large white petals that have a strong fragrance. What would be the most probable pollinating agent for the flower?

(A) Moths
(B) Hummingbirds
(C) Butterflies
(D) Spores
(E) Wind

66. The forelimb of a bat is homologous to the forelimb of a porpoise, meaning that these appendages

(A) perform the same function in both animals
(B) are constructed of bones of the same size and shape
(C) came from widely separated evolutionary lineages
(D) were inherited from a common ancestor and subsequently diverged
(E) arose at the same time in evolutionary history

GO ON TO THE NEXT PAGE

Year	Number of Squirrels
0 (start)	3
1	9
2	28
3	80

67. The data above were collected for a population of squirrels in a forest over the course of 3 years. Which of the graphs below represents these data?

(A)

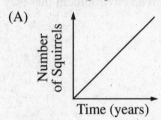

(B)

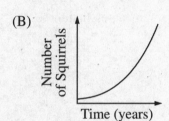

(C)

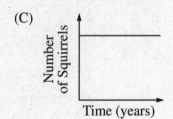

(D)

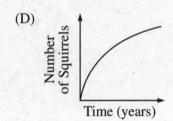

(E)

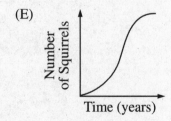

68. The Hawaiian Islands are said to contain the largest number of species of *Drosophila* of any region on Earth. Genetic and biochemical studies suggest that the species are the descendents of a single fertilized female that colonized the islands millions of years ago. All of the following are likely to have contributed to those findings EXCEPT:

(A) Volcanic eruptions and lava flows frequently isolate individual patches of vegetation.
(B) The Hawaiian Islands are very distant from the nearest continent.
(C) The Hawaiian Islands have many plant species found nowhere else on Earth.
(D) The forests of the Hawaiian Islands have identical species composition.
(E) Weather patterns cause the Hawaiian Islands to have a rainy side and a dry side.

69. The seeds of a certain Australian plant are covered with spines that adhere to the feathers of seabirds. A rare color variant of the plant has begun to flourish on a previously unvegetated island. This is an example of which of the following?

(A) Allopatric speciation
(B) Adaptive radiation
(C) Directional selection
(D) Disruptive selection
(E) The founder effect

GO ON TO THE NEXT PAGE

Questions 70-71

A population of *Paramecium caudatum* has the following growth curve on a logarithmic scale.

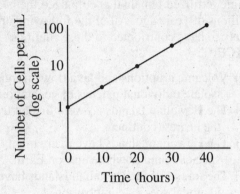

70. The rate of growth of this population is

(A) exponential
(B) additive
(C) stepwise
(D) logistic
(E) hyperbolic

71. The observed pattern of population increase results from growth in an environment that is

(A) deteriorating
(B) patchy
(C) nonlimiting
(D) linear
(E) unpredictable

GO ON TO THE NEXT PAGE

Questions 72-76

In a study of ecological succession, an ecologist measured the rates of photosynthesis of seedlings of three tree species in pots in the laboratory at various light levels. The results are shown in the graph below. Field studies of succession showed that birch trees tended to colonize open areas first. The resulting birch forests tended to be replaced by oak forests, and oak forests tended to be replaced by beech forests.

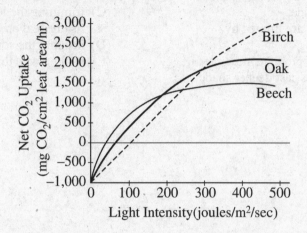

72. At very low light levels, all species show a net loss of CO_2 because

    (A) leaves are shed
    (B) respiratory reactions are reversed
    (C) nitrogen limits plant growth
    (D) respiratory losses exceed photosynthetic gains
    (E) stomates are closed

73. At which of the following light intensities does oak have a higher net rate of CO_2 uptake than do either of the other two species?

    (A)   0 joules/m²/sec
    (B)   50 joules/m²/sec
    (C) 100 joules/m²/sec
    (D) 250 joules/m²/sec
    (E) 350 joules/m²/sec

74. A birch seedling with three leaves of the same size was exposed to 200 joules/m²/second of light. The loss or gain of CO_2 by the plant in one hour is closest to which of the following?

    (A)   0 mg/cm² leaf area
    (B)   300 mg/cm² leaf area
    (C) 1,000 mg/cm² leaf area
    (D) 2,000 mg/cm² leaf area
    (E) 3,000 mg/cm² leaf area

GO ON TO THE NEXT PAGE

75. Which statement about succession is best supported by comparing the data for the three species?

   (A) Late succession species have higher maximum rates of photosynthesis.
   (B) Late succession species are better able to photosynthesize in shade.
   (C) Late succession species are limited by nitrogen.
   (D) Late succession species produce more seeds.
   (E) Early succession species cast deeper shade.

76. All of the following are necessary for obtaining reliable data from this experiment EXCEPT

   (A) holding temperature constant in the laboratory
   (B) keeping illumination consistent among the three species in the laboratory
   (C) trimming the leaves so each plant has the same leaf area
   (D) keeping the soil equally moist in each pot
   (E) using plants that are free of disease

GO ON TO THE NEXT PAGE

Questions 77-80

An experiment was designed to determine the toxicity of the wood preservative pentachlorophenol. Mosquito larvae were placed in beakers of water containing different concentrations of pentachlorophenol.

The larvae were observed and the number alive was determined at the beginning of the experiment and after 24 hours. The percent of larvae remaining alive after 24 hours is shown in the graph below, which represents the average of 3 replicates of each treatment.

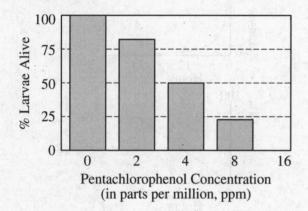

77. Which statement is best supported by the data?

(A) Pentachlorophenol is toxic to mosquito larvae, even in very small amounts.
(B) Pentachlorophenol is lethal to all aquatic life.
(C) Pentachlorophenol acts by blocking cell respiration reactions.
(D) Pentachlorophenol preserves wood by killing fungi and bacteria that cause decay.
(E) The toxicity of pentachlorophenol is inversely proportional to concentration.

78. The experimental design includes all of the following EXCEPT

(A) multiple trials
(B) a control population
(C) dose effect
(D) biological magnification
(E) survival measurements

GO ON TO THE NEXT PAGE

79. The role of the beaker containing 0 parts per million of pentachlorophenol is to

(A) give an estimate of the number of larvae that die without pentachlorophenol
(B) determine the number of larvae that become adults
(C) determine whether water already contains pentachlorophenol
(D) determine the growth rate of larvae in water
(E) provide a supply of larvae to be used in later experiments

80. Using only a concentration of 16 parts per million, a second study is done, collecting data every hour for 24 hours. Which of the following graphs best depicts the expected outcome?

(A)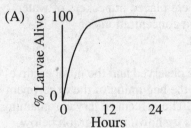

(B)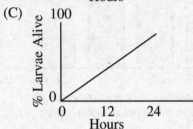

(C)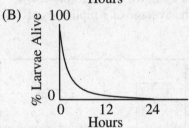

(D)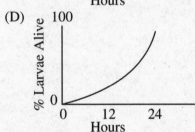

(E)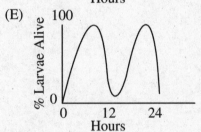

STOP

If you finish before time is called, you may check your work on the entire Biology-E test.

If you are taking the Biology-M test, continue with questions 81-100.
Be sure to start this section of the test by filling in circle 81 on your answer sheet.

Directions: Each of the questions or incomplete statements below is followed by five suggested answers or completions. Some questions pertain to a set that refers to a laboratory or experimental situation. For each question, select the one choice that is the best answer to the question and then fill in the corresponding circle on the answer sheet.

81. When plant cells are placed in a saltwater solution, the volume of the cytoplasm decreases. Which of the following is the best explanation for this observation?

    (A) Cytoplasm leaks out through the cell wall.
    (B) The organelles in the cytoplasm are destroyed as the salt enters the cell.
    (C) The water, especially in the vacuole, leaves the cell.
    (D) Water from outside the cell fills the space between the cell wall and the plasma membrane.
    (E) The nucleus explodes and therefore takes up less space in the cytoplasm.

82. In fruit flies, the allele for red eyes is dominant over the allele for sepia eyes. This trait is not sex-linked. If a heterozygous red-eyed fruit fly mated with a sepia-eyed fruit fly, what percentage of the offspring would have sepia eyes?

    (A)   0%
    (B)   25%
    (C)   50%
    (D)   75%
    (E) 100%

83. An unidentified liquid is isolated from a sample of ground-up bean seeds. When the liquid is added to a test tube of water and shaken vigorously, the water and the unknown liquid separate into two layers after a few minutes. To which class of biological macromolecules should the unknown liquid most likely be assigned?

    (A) Carbohydrates
    (B) Enzymes
    (C) Lipids
    (D) Nucleic acids
    (E) Proteins

84. The secondary and tertiary structures of a protein molecule are ultimately due to which of the following?

    (A) The length of the mRNA molecule being transcribed
    (B) A group of cells specialized to alter protein shape
    (C) A special cellular organelle that fits a protein to its function
    (D) The primary structure (amino acid order) of the protein molecule
    (E) Ionic bonds within the specific amino acid tryptophan

$$ADP + phosphate \rightarrow ATP$$

85. Which of the following biological processes would provide the energy for the reaction above?

    (A) The synthesis of proteins from amino acids
    (B) The combination of glycerol and fatty acids to form a fat
    (C) The combination of glucose and fructose to form sucrose
    (D) The hydrolysis of protein to amino acids
    (E) The oxidation of glucose

86. How many different types of gametes can be produced by an individual who is heterozygous for each of three different genes (e.g., *AaBbCc*), each of which is located on a different chromosome?

    (A)   2
    (B)   4
    (C)   6
    (D)   8
    (E) 16

GO ON TO THE NEXT PAGE

87. In interphase, DNA is observed in which of the following forms?

    (A) Chromosomes aligned at the metaphase plate
    (B) Sister chromatids attached to spindle fibers
    (C) Chromatin
    (D) Tetrads
    (E) Bivalents

88. The rate of exchange of nutrients and water between a living eukaryotic cell and its environment is a function of which of the following properties?

    (A) The ratio of surface area to volume of the cell
    (B) The number of chromosomes
    (C) The rate of DNA transcription in the cell
    (D) The mass of the cell
    (E) The number of organelles in the cell

89. Nondisjunction during meiosis typically results in

    (A) gametes containing an extra chromosome
    (B) gametes having identical DNA
    (C) offspring lacking genetic variation
    (D) cells unable to carry out DNA replication
    (E) circular chromosomes

90. Which of the following combinations of parental genotypes is LEAST likely produce blood type O offspring?

    (A) $I^A i$ and $I^A i$

    (B) $I^B i$ and ii

    (C) ii and $I^A I^B$

    (D) $I^B i$ and $I^B i$

    (E) $I^A i$ and ii

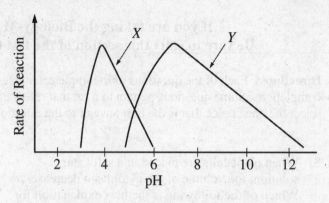

91. The graph above shows the rates of reaction of two enzymes (X and Y) at varying pH levels. Which of the following statements is the best interpretation of this graph?

    (A) Enzyme X has an optimal pH of 6.
    (B) Enzyme X is active over a broader pH range than enzyme Y.
    (C) The optimal pH for enzyme Y is 4.
    (D) Both enzymes X and Y are active between pH 5 and pH 6.
    (E) Enzyme Y works better than enzyme X at higher temperatures.

92. Which of the following is a function of lipids?

    (A) Active transport of ions
    (B) Long-term energy storage
    (C) Oxygen transport
    (D) Transcription
    (E) DNA replication

GO ON TO THE NEXT PAGE

Questions 93-95

Radioactive amino acids were administered to the secretory cells of the pancreas of a guinea pig. Cell samples were then removed at various intervals of time and analyzed for radioactivity in three parts of the cells. The results of the experiment are presented below.

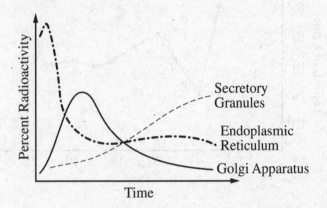

93. Based on the results of the experiment, which of the following molecules would most likely contain the radioactive amino acids?

(A) Phospholipid
(B) Cholesterol
(C) RNA polymerase
(D) Insulin
(E) DNA

94. The experiment was designed to answer which of the following questions?

(A) In what way are cells harmed by radioactivity?
(B) Through what pathway do proteins pass en route to being secreted?
(C) In what cellular organelle is cholesterol inserted into the membrane?
(D) In what cellular organelle are nucleotides polymerized to form nucleic acids?
(E) What is the final extracellular destination of molecules secreted by the pancreas?

95. Which of the following conclusions is supported by the data obtained in the experiment?

(A) The membranes of secretory cells are assembled in the Golgi apparatus.
(B) Amino acids are incorporated into the membrane of the Golgi apparatus.
(C) RNA made in the nucleus is transported to the endoplasmic reticulum, where protein synthesis occurs.
(D) Proteins synthesized on the endoplasmic reticulum are transported to the Golgi apparatus, where they are packaged into secretory vesicles.
(E) Some macromolecules synthesized by the pancreas are secreted into the bloodstream, and others are secreted into ducts leading to the small intestine.

GO ON TO THE NEXT PAGE

Questions 96-97

A hospital patient suffering from a chronic internal infection caused by a bacterium was treated with daily injections of the antibiotic streptomycin (0.5 mg/mL) over a period of 12 days, with the result shown in the figure below.

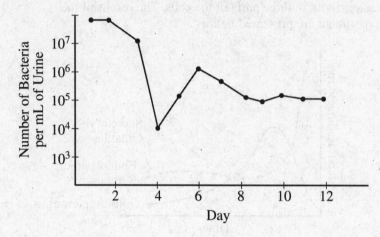

96. How much more bacteria is present per mL of urine on day 12 than on day 4 ?

    (A)   2 times as much
    (B)   5 times as much
    (C)   10 times as much
    (D)   20 times as much
    (E)   100 times as much

97. Which of the following conclusions might be drawn from the data?

    (A) By day 8, the number of bacteria had steadily declined.
    (B) Streptomycin caused a genetic mutation for antibiotic resistance that manifested itself on about day 4.
    (C) Initiating treatment with an alternate antibiotic on day 4 or 5 would have been ineffective in eliminating the bacteria.
    (D) Some of the bacteria that caused the infection were resistant to streptomycin.
    (E) By day 12, the amount of bacteria in the urine had returned to normal.

GO ON TO THE NEXT PAGE

Questions 98-100

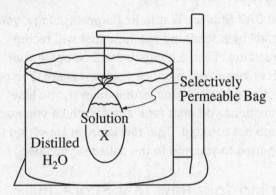

Selectively Permeable Bag

Solution X

Distilled H₂O

Solution X was placed in a bag made of a selectively permeable dialysis membrane. The bag was securely tied, rinsed off with distilled water, and then suspended within a large beaker of distilled water, as shown above. The contents of the bag and the beaker were tested for the presence of sugar, starch, lipid, and protein at the start of the experiment and 24 hours later. The volume of the bag increased during this time. The results of these tests are presented in the table below.

(+ = present; − = absent)

		Start of Experiment	24 hours Later
Contents of Bag	Sugar	+	+
	Starch	+	+
	Lipid	+	+
	Protein	+	+
Contents of Beaker	Sugar	−	+
	Starch	−	−
	Lipid	−	−
	Protein	−	−

98. Which of the following processes accounts for the presence of sugar in the beaker after 24 hours?

(A) Diffusion
(B) Active transport
(C) Pinocytosis
(D) Osmosis
(E) Absorption

99. Which of the following hypotheses is supported by this experiment?

(A) Only organic compounds can move across semipermeable dialysis membranes.
(B) The movement of sugar requires the expenditure of cellular energy.
(C) Starch molecules are smaller than lipid molecules.
(D) Sugar is more soluble in water than is starch.
(E) The movement of molecules across a dialysis membrane depends on molecular size.

100. Correct statements about this experiment include which of the following?

I. There is a net movement of water from the beaker into the bag.
II. Toward the end of the experiment, movement of sugar molecules across the membrane stops.
III. After 24 hours, the solutions in the bag and in the beaker are isotonic.

(A) I only
(B) II only
(C) I and III only
(D) II and III only
(E) I, II, and III

S T O P

IF YOU FINISH BEFORE TIME IS CALLED, YOU MAY CHECK YOUR WORK ON THE ENTIRE BIOLOGY-M TEST. DO NOT TURN TO ANY OTHER TEST IN THIS BOOK.

How to Score the SAT Subject Test in Ecological Biology

When you take an actual SAT Subject Test in Ecological Biology, your answer sheet will be "read" by a scanning machine that will record your response to each question. Then a computer will compare your answers with the correct answers and produce your raw score. You get one point for each correct answer. For each wrong answer, you lose one-fourth of a point. Questions you omit (and any for which you mark more than one answer) are not counted. This raw score is converted to a scaled score that is reported to you and to the colleges you specify.

Worksheet 1. Finding Your Raw Test Score

STEP 1: Table A on the following page lists the correct answers for all the questions on the Subject Test in Ecological Biology that is reproduced in this book. It also serves as a worksheet for you to calculate your raw score.

- Compare your answers with those given in the table.

- Put a check in the column marked "Right" if your answer is correct.

- Put a check in the column marked "Wrong" if your answer is incorrect.

- Leave both columns blank if you omitted the question.

STEP 2: Count the number of right answers.

Enter the total here: _____

STEP 3: Count the number of wrong answers.

Enter the total here: _____

STEP 4: Multiply the number of wrong answers by .250.

Enter the product here: _____

STEP 5: Subtract the result obtained in Step 4 from the total you obtained in Step 2.

Enter the result here: _____

STEP 6: Round the number obtained in Step 5 to the nearest whole number.

Enter the result here: _____

The number you obtained in Step 6 is your raw score.

Answers to Practice Test 1 for Ecological Biology

Table A
Answers to the Subject Test in Ecological Biology - Practice Test 1 and Percentage of Students Answering Each Question Correctly

Question Number	Correct Answer	Right	Wrong	Percent Answering Correctly*	Question Number	Correct Answer	Right	Wrong	Percent Answering Correctly*
1	C			57	26	A			74
2	E			63	27	D			83
3	A			90	28	D			63
4	E			48	29	B			71
5	B			55	30	C			62
6	E			58	31	D			64
7	A			46	32	E			54
8	D			85	33	A			36
9	C			68	34	D			29
10	E			78	35	D			41
11	A			85	36	E			52
12	C			90	37	B			52
13	A			65	38	B			57
14	C			78	39	A			83
15	C			83	40	A			49
16	E			91	41	C			46
17	E			87	42	C			49
18	A			64	43	B			77
19	D			76	44	E			84
20	A			92	45	D			75
21	B			40	46	A			80
22	C			71	47	B			71
23	E			86	48	E			76
24	A			90	49	E			77
25	B			62	50	C			93

Table A continued on next page

Table A continued from previous page

Question Number	Correct Answer	Right	Wrong	Percent Answering Correctly*	Question Number	Correct Answer	Right	Wrong	Percent Answering Correctly*
51	D			85	66	D			77
52	E			54	67	B			82
53	D			55	68	D			30
54	B			62	69	E			35
55	C			83	70	A			46
56	D			61	71	C			54
57	B			69	72	D			60
58	B			55	73	D			90
59	D			70	74	C			67
60	C			77	75	B			42
61	A			53	76	C			60
62	D			38	77	A			73
63	E			73	78	D			62
64	B			85	79	A			80
65	A			60	80	B			92

* These percentages are based on an analysis of the answer sheets for a random sample of 4,188 students who took the original administration of this test and whose mean score was 624. They may be used as an indication of the relative difficulty of a particular question. Each percentage may also be used to predict the likelihood that a typical Subject Test in Ecological Biology candidate will answer correctly that question on this edition of this test.

Note: Answer explanations can be found on page 74.

Finding Your Scaled Score

When you take SAT Subject Tests, the scores sent to the colleges you specify are reported on the College Board scale, which ranges from 200–800. You can convert your practice test score to a scaled score by using Table B. To find your scaled score, locate your raw score in the left-hand column of Table B; the corresponding score in the right-hand column is your scaled score. For example, a raw score of 21 on this particular edition of the Subject Test in Ecological Biology corresponds to a scaled score of 450.

Raw scores are converted to scaled scores to ensure that a score earned on any one edition of a particular Subject Test is comparable to the same scaled score earned on any other edition of the same Subject Test. Because some editions of the tests may be slightly easier or more difficult than others, College Board scaled scores are adjusted so that they indicate the same level of performance regardless of the edition of the test taken and the ability of the group that takes it. Thus, for example, a score of 400 on one edition of a test taken at a particular administration indicates the same level of achievement as a score of 400 on a different edition of the test taken at a different administration.

When you take the SAT Subject Tests during a national administration, your scores are likely to differ somewhat from the scores you obtain on the tests in this book. People perform at different levels at different times for reasons unrelated to the tests themselves. The precision of any test is also limited because it represents only a sample of all the possible questions that could be asked.

Table B
Scaled Score Conversion Table
Subject Test in Ecological Biology - Practice Test 1

Raw Score	Scaled Score	Raw Score	Scaled Score	Raw Score	Scaled Score
80	800	40	570	0	320
79	800	39	570	−1	310
78	800	38	560	−2	310
77	800	37	550	−3	310
76	790	36	550	−4	300
75	790	35	540	−5	300
74	780	34	530	−6	300
73	780	33	530	−7	290
72	770	32	520	−8	290
71	770	31	510	−9	280
70	760	30	510	−10	280
69	760	29	500	−11	280
68	750	28	490	−12	270
67	750	27	490	−13	270
66	740	26	480	−14	260
65	740	25	470	−15	250
64	730	24	470	−16	230
63	720	23	460	−17	220
62	720	22	450	−18	220
61	710	21	450	−19	210
60	700	20	440	−20	210
59	700	19	430		
58	690	18	430		
57	690	17	420		
56	680	16	410		
55	670	15	410		
54	670	14	400		
53	660	13	390		
52	650	12	390		
51	650	11	380		
50	640	10	370		
49	630	9	370		
48	630	8	360		
47	620	7	360		
46	610	6	350		
45	610	5	340		
44	600	4	340		
43	590	3	330		
42	590	2	330		
41	580	1	320		

How Did You Do on the Subject Test in Ecological Biology?

After you score your test and analyze your performance, think about the following questions:

Did you run out of time before reaching the end of the test?

If so, you may need to pace yourself better. For example, maybe you spent too much time on one or two hard questions. A better approach might be to skip the ones you can't answer right away and try answering all the questions that remain on the test. Then if there's time, go back to the questions you skipped.

Did you take a long time reading the directions?

You will save time when you take the test by learning the directions to the Subject Test in Ecological Biology ahead of time. Each minute you spend reading directions during the test is a minute that you could use to answer questions.

How did you handle questions you were unsure of?

If you were able to eliminate one or more of the answer choices as wrong and guess from the remaining ones, your approach probably worked to your advantage. On the other hand, making haphazard guesses or omitting questions without trying to eliminate choices could cost you valuable points.

How difficult were the questions for you compared with other students who took the test?

Table A shows you how difficult the multiple-choice questions were for the group of students who took this test during its national administration. The right-hand column gives the percentage of students that answered each question correctly.

A *question answered correctly by almost everyone in the group is obviously an easier question.* For example, 85 percent of the students answered question 11 correctly. But only 38 percent answered question 62 correctly.

Keep in mind that these percentages are based on just one group of students. They would probably be different with another group of students taking the test.

If you missed several easier questions, go back and try to find out why: Did the questions cover material you haven't yet reviewed? Did you misunderstand the directions?

How to Score the SAT Subject Test in Molecular Biology

When you take an actual SAT Subject Test in Molecular Biology, your answer sheet will be "read" by a scanning machine that will record your response to each question. Then a computer will compare your answers with the correct answers and produce your raw score. You get one point for each correct answer. For each wrong answer, you lose one-fourth of a point. Questions you omit (and any for which you mark more than one answer) are not counted. This raw score is converted to a scaled score that is reported to you and to the colleges you specify.

Worksheet 1. Finding Your Raw Test Score

STEP 1: Table A on the following page lists the correct answers for all the questions on the Subject Test in Molecular Biology that is reproduced in this book. It also serves as a worksheet for you to calculate your raw score.

- Compare your answers with those given in the table.

- Put a check in the column marked "Right" if your answer is correct.

- Put a check in the column marked "Wrong" if your answer is incorrect.

- Leave both columns blank if you omitted the question.

STEP 2: Count the number of right answers.

Enter the total here: _____

STEP 3: Count the number of wrong answers.

Enter the total here: _____

STEP 4: Multiply the number of wrong answers by .250.

Enter the product here: _____

STEP 5: Subtract the result obtained in Step 4 from the total you obtained in Step 2.

Enter the result here: _____

STEP 6: Round the number obtained in Step 5 to the nearest whole number.

Enter the result here: _____

The number you obtained in Step 6 is your raw score.

Answers to Practice Test 1 for Molecular Biology

Table A
Answers to the Subject Test in Molecular Biology - Practice Test 1 and Percentage of Students Answering
Each Question Correctly

Question Number	Correct Answer	Right	Wrong	Percent Answering Correctly*	Question Number	Correct Answer	Right	Wrong	Percent Answering Correctly*
1	C			69	26	A			78
2	E			77	27	D			85
3	A			94	28	D			73
4	E			63	29	B			73
5	B			63	30	C			64
6	E			61	31	D			75
7	A			55	32	E			58
8	D			89	33	A			47
9	C			71	34	D			36
10	E			83	35	D			46
11	A			84	36	E			59
12	C			89	37	B			62
13	A			66	38	B			56
14	C			78	39	A			84
15	C			89	40	A			53
16	E			94	41	C			57
17	E			93	42	C			57
18	A			67	43	B			81
19	D			85	44	E			87
20	A			96	45	D			79
21	B			49	46	A			88
22	C			77	47	B			80
23	E			88	48	E			84
24	A			92	49	E			82
25	B			74	50	C			95

Table A continued on next page

Table A continued from previous page

Question Number	Correct Answer	Right	Wrong	Percent Answering Correctly*	Question Number	Correct Answer	Right	Wrong	Percent Answering Correctly*
51	D			89	86	D			54
52	E			60	87	C			77
53	D			62	88	A			82
54	B			71	89	A			81
55	C			87	90	C			86
56	D			71	91	D			84
57	B			77	92	B			92
58	B			54	93	D			51
59	D			72	94	B			61
60	C			81	95	D			70
81	C			86	96	C			88
82	C			88	97	D			53
83	C			85	98	A			82
84	D			64	99	E			78
85	E			66	100	A			51

* These percentages are based on an analysis of the answer sheets for a random sample of 8,445 students who took the original administration of this test and whose mean score was 655. They may be used as an indication of the relative difficulty of a particular question. Each percentage may also be used to predict the likelihood that a typical Subject Test in Molecular Biology candidate will answer correctly that question on this edition of this test.

Note: Answer explanations can be found on page 74.

Finding Your Scaled Score

When you take SAT Subject Tests, the scores sent to the colleges you specify are reported on the College Board scale, which ranges from 200-800. You can convert your practice test score to a scaled score by using Table B. To find your scaled score, locate your raw score in the left-hand column of Table B; the corresponding score in the right-hand column is your scaled score. For example, a raw score of 21 on this particular edition of the Subject Test in Molecular Biology corresponds to a scaled score of 450.

Raw scores are converted to scaled scores to ensure that a score earned on any one edition of a particular Subject Test is comparable to the same scaled score earned on any other edition of the same Subject Test. Because some editions of the tests may be slightly easier or more difficult than others, College Board scaled scores are adjusted so that they indicate the same level of performance regardless of the edition of the test taken and the ability of the group that takes it. Thus, for example, a score of 400 on one edition of a test taken at a particular administration indicates the same level of achievement as a score of 400 on a different edition of the test taken at a different administration.

When you take the SAT Subject Tests during a national administration, your scores are likely to differ somewhat from the scores you obtain on the tests in this book. People perform at different levels at different times for reasons unrelated to the tests themselves. The precision of any test is also limited because it represents only a sample of all the possible questions that could be asked.

Table B
Scaled Score Conversion Table
Subject Test in Molecular Biology - Practice Test 1

Raw Score	Scaled Score	Raw Score	Scaled Score	Raw Score	Scaled Score
80	800	40	570	0	320
79	800	39	560	−1	310
78	800	38	560	−2	310
77	790	37	550	−3	310
76	790	36	540	−4	300
75	780	35	540	−5	300
74	780	34	530	−6	290
73	770	33	530	−7	290
72	770	32	520	−8	290
71	760	31	510	−9	280
70	750	30	510	−10	280
69	750	29	500	−11	280
68	740	28	500	−12	270
67	730	27	490	−13	270
66	730	26	480	−14	260
65	720	25	480	−15	240
64	710	24	470	−16	240
63	710	23	460	−17	230
62	700	22	460	−18	220
61	690	21	450	−19	210
60	690	20	440	−20	200
59	680	19	440		
58	680	18	430		
57	670	17	420		
56	660	16	420		
55	660	15	410		
54	650	14	400		
53	650	13	390		
52	640	12	390		
51	630	11	380		
50	630	10	370		
49	620	9	370		
48	620	8	360		
47	610	7	350		
46	600	6	350		
45	600	5	340		
44	590	4	340		
43	590	3	330		
42	580	2	330		
41	570	1	320		

How Did You Do on the Subject Test in Molecular Biology?

After you score your test and analyze your performance, think about the following questions:

Did you run out of time before reaching the end of the test?

If so, you may need to pace yourself better. For example, maybe you spent too much time on one or two hard questions. A better approach might be to skip the ones you can't answer right away and try answering all the questions that remain on the test. Then if there's time, go back to the questions you skipped.

Did you take a long time reading the directions?

You will save time when you take the test by learning the directions to the Subject Test in Molecular Biology ahead of time. Each minute you spend reading directions during the test is a minute that you could use to answer questions.

How did you handle questions you were unsure of?

If you were able to eliminate one or more of the answer choices as wrong and guess from the remaining ones, your approach probably worked to your advantage. On the other hand, making haphazard guesses or omitting questions without trying to eliminate choices could cost you valuable points.

How difficult were the questions for you compared with other students who took the test?

Table A shows you how difficult the multiple-choice questions were for the group of students who took this test during its national administration. The right-hand column gives the percentage of students that answered each question correctly.

A *question answered correctly by almost everyone in the group is obviously an easier question.* For example, 84 percent of the students answered question 11 correctly. But only 54 percent answered question 86 correctly.

Keep in mind that these percentages are based on just one group of students. They would probably be different with another group of students taking the test.

If you missed several easier questions, go back and try to find out why: Did the questions cover material you haven't yet reviewed? Did you misunderstand the directions?

Answer Explanations

For Practice Test 1

Question 1

Choice (C) is the correct answer. Mitochondria are membrane-bound organelles found in eukaryotic organisms, including plants and animals. Prokaryotic organisms do not have membrane-bound organelles.

Question 2

Choice (E) is the correct answer. Ribosomes are found in cells of all living organisms. This includes cells of both prokaryotes and eukaryotes (including plants and animals.)

Question 3

Choice (A) is the correct answer. Cell walls containing cellulose are found in plants but not in animals or prokaryotes. (Note that while there are some unicellular eukaryotic organisms that have cell walls containing cellulose, that is not given as an option.)

Question 4

Choice (E) is the correct answer. In all organisms, the cytosol is contained within the cell or plasma membrane. This includes prokaryotes and eukaryotes such as plants and animals.

Question 5

Choice (B) is the correct answer. In mammals, the blastocyst (an early embryonic stage) implants in the uterus, where development continues. The epididymis and testes are structures found in males. Implantation in the oviduct does not normally result in successful gestation. The ovary releases the egg before fertilization.

Question 6

Choice (E) is the correct answer. The mammalian testes typically produce sperm (spermatogenesis) from the time the animal enters puberty until its death. Gametogenesis in the ovary ends with menopause in humans and a similar cessation of fertility in some other mammals. Gametogenesis does not occur in the other structures listed.

Question 7

Choice (A) is the correct answer. Fertilization in mammals occurs in the oviduct. In humans, the oviducts are also termed the Fallopian tubes. Fertilization in the male structures (epididymis and testes) is not possible. The ovary releases the egg before fertilization. Fertilization in the uterus does not normally result in successful gestation.

Question 8

Choice (D) is the correct answer. If individuals choose mates based on a phenotypic trait, mating is not random, so condition D is not met. The other conditions are not affected.

Question 9

Choice (C) is the correct answer. If a new nucleotide sequence appears in the gene pool, there is a new mutation, so condition C is not met. The other conditions are not affected.

Question 10

Choice (E) is the correct answer. If individuals with certain genotypes exhibit differential survival, they are better adapted to their environment and thus are experiencing natural selection, so condition E is not met. The other conditions are not affected.

Question 11

Choice (A) is the correct answer. Mainland species are more likely to become established on islands closer to the mainland (A and D). The island that is largest likely has more available niches, making option A a better choice than option D.

Question 12

Choice (C) is the correct answer. Island C is farthest from the mainland and therefore is expected to have the lowest immigration rate of these five islands.

Question 13

Choice (A) is the correct answer. Island A is expected to have the lowest extinction rate because it is nearest to the mainland, with greater opportunity for reintroduction of species by migration, and is expected to have greater habitat diversity due to its larger size, allowing for survival of specialized species.

Question 14

Choice (C) is the correct answer. Island C is farthest from the mainland and also smaller than the other islands. The migration of species from the mainland is less likely on this island than on the others, and the number of available niches is expected to be smaller due to the smaller size of the island, so it is likely to have the smallest number of species.

Question 15

Choice (C) is the correct answer. Human blood is slightly basic and generally ranges from pH 7.35 to pH 7.45. Of the options given, it is closest to pH 7.5.

Question 16

Choice (E) is the correct answer. One way to determine if an individual is heterozygous for a trait is to perform a test cross, which is to cross it with a known homozygous recessive individual. Option E describes a test cross and is the best option of the five given to determine if the black guinea pig is heterozygous for fur color. Option A is incorrect because there would not be any white hairs present if the black allele is completely dominant to the white allele. Option B is incorrect because the structure of the follicle is not responsible for the difference in hair color. Option C is incorrect because chemically analyzing the messenger RNA would not indicate whether the recessive allele is present. Option D is incorrect because examining the chromosomes in the salivary glands will not indicate whether the recessive allele is present.

Question 17

Choice (E) is the correct answer. Crossing-over is the exchange of pieces of chromatids from two homologous chromosomes during synapsis of prophase I of meiosis. The exchange results in increased genetic variation in the offspring by rearranging the genetic material inherited from the two parents. Options A, B, C, and D do not represent an exchange of segments between homologous chromosomes.

Question 18

Choice (A) is the correct answer. Endotherms generate heat from metabolic reactions. Ectotherms are primarily dependent on external heat sources. Option B is incorrect because endotherms can have body temperatures that are lower than the ambient temperature. Option C is incorrect because endotherms do not always have a higher body temperature than ectotherms have. In a very hot climate, ectotherms might have a higher body temperature than the endotherms have. Option D is incorrect because some ectotherms have behavioral methods of regulating body temperature, such as basking in the sun. Option E is incorrect because endotherms can typically perform vigorous activity for longer periods of time than endotherms can.

Question 19

Choice (D) is the correct answer. Incomplete dominance is exhibited by the pink flowers, which are heterozygous. The offspring resulting from the cross of two pink-flowered plants show the genotypic ratio of 1 homozygous dominant to 2 heterozygous to 1 homozygous recessive. The homozygous dominant plants have red flowers, the homozygous recessive plants have white flowers, and the heterozygous plants have pink flowers. The other options represent inheritance patterns that do not result in a 1:2:1 ratio.

Question 20

Choice (A) is the correct answer. The Punnett square shows a cross between two heterozygous individuals, both with the genotype *Gg*. The genotypic ratio predicted from this cross is 1 *GG*: 2 *Gg*: 1 *gg*. Since green is dominant, an individual with one or two copies of the dominant allele, *G*, will be green; thus, the phenotypic ratio is 3 green : 1 yellow, or 25 percent yellow. There is no evidence to suggest that 25 percent will not survive (option B), and the ratios in options C, D, and E are not correct.

Question 21

Choice (B) is the correct answer. The molecule formed from one adenine molecule, one ribose molecule, and one phosphate group is a nucleotide. Amino acids (A) are comprised of a carboxyl group, an amino group, a central carbon, and a side group, ATP (C) has three phosphate groups, RNA (D) is composed of many nucleotides, and DNA (E) is composed of many nucleotides with deoxyribose sugars.

Question 22

Choice (C) is the correct answer. Atmospheric nitrogen must be converted into a form that is usable by living organisms. Bacteria convert the free nitrogen to ammonia, which is then converted into a form that plants can use. It is not converted directly into DNA (option A) or amino acids (option E), and it cannot be changed into other elements (oxygen in option B, or carbon and hydrogen in option D).

Question 23

Choice (E) is the correct answer. Fungi do <u>not</u> produce seed-containing fruit. Seed-containing fruits are produced by flowering plants (angiosperms). Note that this question is asking for the one option that is not true: options A, B, C, and D are all characteristics of fungi; only E is <u>not</u> a characteristic of fungi.

Question 24

Choice (A) is the correct answer. The symbiotic relationship that is beneficial to both species is mutualism. In commensalism (B), one organism benefits and one is unaffected. In neutralism (C), neither benefits. In parasitism (D), one organisms benefits (the parasite) and the other is harmed (the host). Likewise in predation (E), one organism benefits (the predator) and the other is harmed (the prey).

Question 25

Choice (B) is the correct answer. The process of sexual reproduction results in offspring that are genetically different from the parents. In multicellular organisms, haploid gametes are produced in diploid individuals via meiosis. Fertilization results when two gametes unite, producing a new diploid individual. Option A is incorrect because eggs and sperm can be motile or nonmotile. Option C is incorrect because zygotes are formed from the union of two gametes, not by the process of mitosis. Option D is incorrect because it suggests that the gamete has 4 chromosomes total in two pairs making it a diploid cell. Also, each species has a set number of chromosomes which is generally more than 4. Option E is incorrect because centrioles are not found in all multicellular organisms.

Question 26

Choice (A) is the correct answer. Endosperm is a tissue found in the seeds of most flowering plants that provides stored energy for the developing plant embryo. Yolk is found in eggs and supplies energy for the developing animal embryo. Option B is incorrect because plants do not contain yolk. Option C is incorrect because yolk is not triploid. Option D is incorrect because neither functions to discourage predation. Option E is incorrect because neither is produced by the male parent.

Question 27

Choice (D) is the correct answer. The fossil record shows that prokaryotic bacteria appeared on Earth before the other organisms listed—ferns (A), mosses (B), fungi (C), and lichens (E)—which are all eukaryotes. Lichens are unusual in that they are a composite of eukaryotic organisms that consists of: an alga and one or more types of fungus.

Question 28

Choice (D) is the correct answer. Deoxygenated blood moves from the right atrium to the right ventricle to the lungs, where it is oxygenated. Then the oxygenated blood returns to the heart and enters the left atrium. It then moves to the left ventricle, which pumps it out to the body via the aorta. Options A to D present the steps in the wrong order.

Question 29

Choice (B) is the correct answer. Carbon dioxide is considered to be a greenhouse gas, which is a gas that traps heat in the atmosphere. Rising levels in historical and recent times due to human activities have led to an increase in average global temperatures. Option A is incorrect because CO_2 does not thin the atmosphere. Option C is incorrect because CO_2 does not destroy ozone. Option D is incorrect because forest fires are not the main cause of global warming. Option E is also incorrect because increased CO_2 will not enable more shortwave radiation to reach Earth's surface.

Question 30

Choice (C) is the correct answer. Since the disease is rare, it is most likely that the father is heterozygous. Since there is no history of the disease in the mother's family, it is likely that she does not have the deleterious allele. The young man, therefore, has a 50 percent chance of inheriting the dominant allele from his father and developing the disease. The remaining options give incorrect probabilities.

Question 31

Choice (D) is the correct answer. The hormone that is involved in the regulation of water conservation in humans and other mammals is antidiuretic hormone (ADH). Follicle-stimulating hormone (FSH) (A) regulates reproductive processes among other processes; insulin (B) regulates blood glucose levels; prolactin (C) regulates the production of milk; and oxytocin (E) regulates the progression of labor during childbirth, as well as other physiological responses.

Question 32

Choice (E) is the correct answer. Note that this question is asking for the least useful evidence. Dietary requirements (E) would provide the least amount of information on evolutionary relationships, and hence is the best choice. In constructing a phylogenetic tree showing the relationships of mammals, fossils (A), nucleotide sequences (B), amino acid sequences (C), and tooth structure (D) would all be useful.

Question 33

Choice (A) is the correct answer. The movement of solutes into guard cells causes water to move into the guard cells by osmosis, which then causes the stomata to open. Among the solutes that are taken up by guard cells are potassium ions. Option B is incorrect because the inflow of ions will not cause the guard cells to shrink, and when the guard cells shrink, the stomata close. Option C is incorrect because the inflow of ions changes the osmolarity of the cytosol. Option D is incorrect because the inflow of ions does not disrupt the membrane. Option E is incorrect because the inflow of ions does not change the water channels.

Question 34

Choice (D) is the correct answer. Lymph is the fluid in the lymphatic system. It is similar to blood plasma but may contain some white blood cells, and it is not contained in a closed system. Option A is incorrect because lymph does not contain red blood cells and platelets. Option B is incorrect because lymph does not contain erythrocytes (red blood cells) that have leaked out of blood vessels. Option C is incorrect because antihistamines are medications that block histamine-induced inflammation and are not contained in lymph. Option E is incorrect because lymph is not produced at lymph nodes.

Question 35

Choice (D) is the correct answer. Animals with one opening to the digestive tract and two layers of tissues belong to the phylum Cnidaria, which includes jellyfish, corals, and anemones, and are illustrated in figures II and IV. Figure I is an earthworm, which belongs to the phylum Annelida. Figure III is a sea star, which belongs to the phylum Echinodermata.

Question 36

Choice (E) is the correct answer. The scar will remain at the same height on the tree trunk, 0.90 meter above the ground, because the vertical growth of the tree occurs only at the ends of the shoots or branches. The trunk will increase in diameter, but this will not affect the vertical position.

Question 37

Choice (B) is the correct answer. Alleles are alternate forms of the same gene. Different alleles may code for proteins with different amino acid sequences. Option A is incorrect because the nucleotide sequences, though similar, are not identical. Option C and D are incorrect because alleles of a single gene are found at the same location on homologous chromosomes. Option E is incorrect because different copies of the gene (different alleles) are located on different chromosomes, not on complementary strands of the DNA molecule that comprises one chromosome.

Question 38

Choice (B) is the correct answer. DDT is a pesticide that has long-lasting environmental effects. It accumulates in body fat and exhibits a biomagnification effect, with apex predators accumulating more DDT in their tissues than other organisms in the same environment do. DDT accumulation in birds of prey led to weak egg shells, which led to population declines in many species. DDT is currently banned in the United States. It is not harmful to plants (A), does not leach nitrogen (C), does not harm the ozone layer (D), and does not serve as food for harmful bacteria (E).

Question 39

Choice (A) is the correct answer. Iridium is rare on Earth, but as it is found in meteorites in more abundance, the discovery of a layer of iridium-enriched rock has been used as evidence supporting the extinction of the dinosaurs because of a meteor impact. Options B, C, D, and E would not result in a worldwide deposit of iridium.

Question 40

Choice (A) is the correct answer. Among the adaptations that enabled vertebrate animals to be successful in terrestrial environments are lungs, kidneys, and amniotic eggs. Lungs permit breathing of air to obtain oxygen; efficient kidneys help to retain water and maintain homeostasis; and amniotic eggs do not require external water to maintain a wet environment around the developing embryos. The other options include characteristics found in all vertebrates (ovaries and testes, backbone, waterproof skin, closed circulator system), and some (teeth, four-chambered heart, scales, binocular vision, wings) found in select groups that are not found in the vertebrates that colonized early terrestrial habitats.

Question 41

Choice (C) is the correct answer. Sons inherit an X chromosome from their mother and a Y chromosome from their father. The mother has 2 X chromosomes, one of which has the allele for color blindness, which she inherited from her father. In this case, the father would contribute a Y chromosome to the son, and the mother would have equal probability of contributing the X chromosome for normal color vision or the X chromosome with the allele for color blindness to any of her sons. The other options all give the wrong probability.

Question 42

Choice (C) is the correct answer. If an organism is homozygous for an allele that encodes a defective digestive enzyme, it will not produce that enzyme and thus metabolic functions will be affected and homeostasis compromised. Options A and B are incorrect, as the enzyme will not be produced at all. Option D is incorrect, as the organism would not have an increased susceptibility to mutations. Option E is incorrect, as evolution will not occur at a faster rate.

Question 43

Choice (B) is the correct answer. The largest area with no bacterial growth is found in quadrant 3, which contained the paper disk soaked in tetracycline. The other quadrants showed less antibacterial effect (A, C, and D), and we have no information on using two antibiotics together (E).

Question 44

Choice (E) is the correct answer. The best explanation for the growth of some bacteria within the area of no growth around the paper disk soaked in penicillin is that there are some bacteria present that have resistance to penicillin. Option A is not supported by the data, as only one medium is used. Option B is also not supported by the data. The data show that penicillin is less effective against this particular bacterium than the other antibiotics used, but that it still has an antibiotic effect. Option C is not supported by the data. Option D is also not supported by the data, as the colonies were not found in the no-growth areas in all quadrants.

Question 45

Choice (D) is the correct answer. The experiment is testing the effects of four antibiotics. A good control will keep everything constant except the presence of antibiotic. Therefore, the best control for this experiment would be use of the same nutrient agar, the same strain of bacteria, and a paper disk with no antibiotics on it. Options A, B, C, and E are not correct because they would not allow the experimenter to be certain the effects seen were due only to the presence of antibiotic.

Question 46

Choice (A) is the correct answer. The letters "A," "T," "G," and "C" stand for the nucleotides adenine, thymine, guanine, and cytosine. Options B, C, D, and E are not correct.

Question 47

Choice (B) is the correct answer. If the individual must have two copies of the sequence of nucleotides in order to exhibit a particular condition, the condition must be recessive. If it were dominant (A), the condition would be exhibited with a single copy of sequence II (E). There is no information that would support sex linkage (C) or codominance (D).

Question 48

Choice (E) is the correct answer. Since sequence II is missing one nucleotide triplet, it will therefore produce mRNA with one fewer codon and thus a protein with one fewer amino acid. Options A, B, C, and D describe different types of mutant proteins but not the one that is produced by sequence II.

Question 49

Choice (E) is the correct answer. A comparison of the two sequences indicates that sequence II differs from sequence I at the third triplet. The triplet AAA is missing, indicating a deletion. Options A, B, C, and D describe different types of mutations but not the one that is seen in sequence II. A frameshift mutation can result from insertions or deletions. A substitution mutation is when one base is substituted for another, which may or may not result in a different amino acid in the protein produced. An inversion mutation is when a set of nucleotides is flipped. A translocation is when a piece of one chromosome changes position on the chromosome or is inserted into a nonhomologous chromosome.

Question 50

Choice (C) is the correct answer. The average radicle length is longest in group 3, which was maintained at pH 7. The other options represent growth at pH levels that resulted in shorter radicles.

Question 51

Choice (D) is the correct answer. The independent (manipulated) variable in the experiment is the pH of the aqueous solutions used. The other options identify factors that were held constant (A, B, and E) or the dependent (measured) variable (C).

Question 52

Choice (E) is the correct answer. Note that this question asks for the response that is <u>not</u> true; options A, B, C, and D are true statements about germination. Option E is the statement that is not true about radicle growth. Light, whether low or high level, is not required for germination. Light is required after germination for photosynthesis.

Question 53

Choice (D) is the correct answer. The plants were maintained under the same conditions of light and temperature (i.e., light and temperature were controlled). Options that include only one of these (A and B) or options that include pH, which was <u>not</u> kept constant (C and E) are incorrect.

Question 54

Choice (B) is the correct answer. Neuron n is a motor neuron that innervates muscle segment I. Under normal conditions, neuron p, a sensory neuron, sends a signal into Ganglion I, where it is received and transmitted to neuron n. If neuron n is destroyed, there will be no response, so the muscular contraction in segment I would not be initiated. Option A is not correct because the motor neuron does not sense stimuli at the skin. Option C is not correct because the motor neuron to segment II has not been destroyed and there is no transmission of information from segment I to segment II. There is no information suggesting that other neurons would be destroyed (D and E) as a result of the loss of neuron n.

Question 55

Choice (C) is the correct answer. If the worm is touched at segment III, the stimulus will be received by sensory neuron w, then transmitted to neuron u, and finally to motor neuron v for the response. The other options include neurons that are not part of this stimulus-response pathway. Other segments will likely response via the connections between ganglion III and the other ganglia, but the question asks only about contraction of segment III.

Question 56

Choice (D) is the correct answer. If the worm is touched at segment III, the stimulus will be received by sensory neuron w, and then for a response to occur in segment II, motor neuron q must be involved. The neuron connecting w and q is t. All of the other choices can be eliminated because they do not include both neurons w and q.

Question 57

Choice (B) is the correct answer. If neuron y in ganglion IV is destroyed, there will be no communication between segments I and III. Options A, C, and E are all incorrect because they involve the communication within the same segment. Option D is incorrect because segments II and III have a pathway for communication via neuron t.

Question 58

Choice (B) is the correct answer. The diagram shows the stages of primary succession in a terrestrial ecosystem. In primary succession, the first colonizers are typically lichens, which form on the bare rocks. The other options do not describe organisms that typically colonize bare-rock during primary succession.

Question 59

Choice (D) is the correct answer. In succession, the species in each stage alter the environment in such a way that makes it more hospitable for the species in the next stage. Option A is incorrect because there is ample sunlight for the pioneer species. Option B is incorrect because there is very little or no soil available to the colonizing species (lichens), not because of the pH. Option C is incorrect because the colonizing species do not inhibit the growth of the pioneer species by secreting chemicals. Option E is incorrect because the plants at later stages of succession are different species, not a single species that accumulates mutations.

Question 60

Choice (C) is the correct answer. The mature forest pictured is typical of a temperate deciduous forest. Tall trees would be lacking in the tundra (A) and the desert (E) biomes; chaparral (D) would be primarily grassland, and taiga or coniferous forest (B) would have mostly coniferous trees (e.g., pines, firs, hemlocks).

Question 61

Choice (A) is the correct answer. Members of the phylum Porifera do not have true tissues. The node that separates them from other animals is node A.

Question 62

Choice (D) is the correct answer. The deuterostomes include the echinoderms and the chordates. The node that separates them from the protostomes is node D. Protostomes include mollusks, annelids, and arthropods. These terms refer to embryological development. In protostomes, the blastopore develops into the mouth, and in deuterostomes it develops into the anus.

Question 63

Choice (E) is the correct answer. The bony endoskeleton of vertebrates has several functions. It protects some of the internal organs, such as the heart, lungs, and brain; it acts as a site for muscle attachment; and it serves as a reservoir of calcium, helping to maintain homeostasis. The other options do not include all of these functions.

Question 64

Choice (B) is the correct answer. Sexual reproduction in all organisms results in increased genetic variation in the offspring, so this is true for flowering plants as well. Genetically identical offspring (A) are typically produced via asexual reproduction. Mutation rates (C) are not affected by the mode of reproduction, and plant height (D) and photosynthetic output (E) cannot be predicted from the mode of reproduction.

Question 65

Choice (A) is the correct answer. Moths are the most probable pollinating agent of a night-blooming, fragrant flower. Hummingbirds (B) and butterflies (C) are active during the day; flowers do not use spores (D) to reproduce; and a wind-pollinated plant (E) would not invest in flowers with a fragrance or color, nor would they open specifically at night.

Question 66

Choice (D) is the correct answer. Homologous structures are defined as those that have similar characteristics due to shared ancestry. The forelimbs of a bat and a porpoise contain similar bones, inherited from their common ancestor, even though the appendages have very different appearances and functions. Analogous structures are similar in appearance or function, but not because of shared ancestry. Option A is incorrect because homologous structures may or may not perform the same function. Option B is incorrect because the bones do not have to be the same size and shape. Option C is incorrect because if they came from widely separated evolutionary lineages, they would not share a recent common ancestor; this might be an example of convergence. Option E is incorrect because the time a structure appeared is not evidence of shared ancestry.

Question 67

Choice (B) is the correct answer. The data show the population increasing each year by a factor of approximately 3. There is a large increase between year 1 and year 2, and then another large increase between year 2 and year 3. The graph that best shows the rapid increase is B. The other options do not reflect the data in the table.

Question 68

Choice (D) is the correct answer. The large number of *Drosophila* species in the Hawaiian Islands is due to adaptive radiation. There are many different environments on the islands and no gene flow from the mainland due to the great distance. Options A, B, C, and E all offer reasons for the diversity of the insects. Option D, even if true, would not contribute to adaptive radiation, as a uniform habitat would not lead to strong selective pressure on the species that are present.

Question 69

Choice (E) is the correct answer. It is most likely that the seeds were carried to the previously unvegetated island by the seabirds. Since the color variant on this island is rare in other places, it is most likely present on the islands due to a random colonization event. The founder effect occurs when a new population arises from only a few members of the original population. The small size of the founding population leads to reduced genetic variation in the new population. Option A is incorrect because allopatric speciation occurs when populations are separated geographically. Option B is incorrect because adaptive radiation occurs when organisms diversify from an ancestral species into many new species. Option C is incorrect because directional selection occurs in response to selective pressure on a phenotype. Option D is incorrect because disruptive selection occurs when selective pressure favors different extreme phenotypes over the intermediate form.

Question 70

Choice (A) is the correct answer. The X axis has a logarithmic scale; each gradation represents a factor of 10. The line is straight, but due to the log scale it is actually increasing exponentially. All of the other options would describe lines with different shapes.

Question 71

Choice (C) is the correct answer. Populations that increase exponentially generally do not have any limiting factors, such as nutrients, or nesting sites. Once these factors become limited in supply, the growth rate of the population will decline.

Question 72

Choice (D) is the correct answer. In all cases, the species show a net loss of CO_2 at low light intensity because the CO_2 released in cellular respiration exceeds the amount of CO_2 fixed in photosynthesis. The low light levels are insufficient to maintain high levels of photosynthesis.

Question 73

Choice (D) is the correct answer. The graph shows the solid line for the oak tree to be higher than that of the other species at approximately 250 joules/m²/sec. The question asks about the point at which the oak tree has a higher net uptake of CO_2 than either of the other species have, not when it is highest or which tree has the highest net uptake.

Question 74

Choice (C) is the correct answer. The graph shows that at 200 joules/m²/sec, the net CO_2 uptake is close to 1,000 mg/cm². Note that this uptake is given as an average over the leaf area per hour, so the number of leaves, or total area, is irrelevant.

Question 75

Choice (B) is the correct answer. We are told in the introductory paragraph that birch trees are early colonizers and that birch forests are replaced by oak forests, which are then replaced by beech forests. The graph shows that at low light intensity, the late-succession beech trees have a higher CO_2 uptake (indicating photosynthetic activity) than the other species have.

Question 76

Choice (C) is the correct answer. Note that the correct answer is the option that does not need to be kept constant. In the laboratory, conditions such as temperature (A), soil moisture levels (D), illumination levels (B), and health and number of plants (E) should all be controlled. Different leaf areas will not affect the measurement, since CO_2 uptake is given per unit area.

Question 77

Choice (A) is the correct answer. The data show that at levels of 2 parts per million, pentachlorophenol kills nearly 25% of the mosquito larvae. The effect increases substantially with greater concentrations, but it can be concluded that it is toxic to mosquito larvae in small amounts. Options B, C, and D are not addressed or supported by the data. Option E is incorrect because the impact of pentachlorophenol on mosquito larvae increases with increasing concentration.

Question 78

Choice (D) is the correct answer. Note that the correct answer is the one that was not part of the study. There were three replicates (A): a treatment group with no pesticide (B), the measurement of dose effect (C), and survival measurements, reported as % alive after each treatment (E). Biological magnification (D), is the process by which substances accumulate in the bodies of organisms at higher trophic levels. This is not part of the study, so it is the correct answer.

Question 79

Choice (A) is the correct answer. The beaker with 0 parts per million of pentachlorophenol is the control beaker for the experiment. The control treatment allows the researchers to attribute lethality in the other samples to pentachlorophenol and not to another component in the experiment.

Question 80

Choice (B) is the correct answer. The question is asking for a prediction of the effect of 16 parts per million concentration of pentachlorophenol on the mosquito larvae during 24 hours of exposure. The original experiment showed that at 16 ppm there were no surviving larvae after 24 hours. Graph B shows a rapid drop in the percent of larvae alive and very few alive after 24 hours. Graphs A, C, and D all show 100 percent of the larvae alive at the end of 24 hours, which is not reasonable, and graph E is unreasonable because it has the number of larvae alive decreasing and then increasing again.

Question 81

Choice (C) is the correct answer. When a cell is placed in a solution that has a greater concentration of solutes, or salt in this case, the water inside the cell moves out of the cell by osmosis. The plant cell would retain its general shape due to the rigid cell wall, but the volume of the cytoplasm will decrease. The cytoplasm (A) cannot cross an intact cell membrane, nor can the salt (B). Water from outside the cell (D) will not enter against the concentration gradient and does not remain in the space between the cell wall and plasma membrane, and the nucleus (E) does not explode when water is lost from the cell.

Question 82

Choice (C) is the correct answer. The heterozygous red-eyed fly has one allele for red eyes and one allele for sepia eyes. The homozygous sepia-eyed fly has two sepia alleles. The sepia-eyed fly will pass on a sepia allele to its offspring, and the red-eyed fly can pass on either a red-eye allele or a sepia-eye allele with equal probability, which will result in 50 percent of the offspring having either phenotype. The other options give incorrect percentages.

Question 83

Choice (C) is the correct answer. We are told that the liquid added to water separates into two layers. Lipids do not dissolve in water and will separate into two layers when mixed with water. The other substances listed (A, B, D, E) will dissolve in water.

Question 84

Choice (D) is the correct answer. The primary structure of a protein is the amino acid sequence. The secondary and tertiary structures give the protein its three-dimensional shape. The three-dimensional shape is created by internal bonding and/or attractions between atoms on different amino acids. The ultimate determiner of the secondary and tertiary structure of a protein is the initial amino acid sequence or the primary structure. The length (A) of the protein does not determine the shape, and groups of cells (B) or special organelles (C) are not required for this self-assembly process. Tryptophan (E) has a hydrophobic side chain, not an electrically charged group.

Question 85

Choice (E) is the correct answer. The reaction shown is the addition of a phosphate group to a molecule of ADP (adenosine diphosphate) to form ATP (adenosine triphosphate). This reaction requires energy.

Options A, B, and C are all synthesis reactions that require energy; they are not energy-producing reactions. Option D is a reaction that breaks down a macromolecule, but it does not release enough energy to drive the reaction shown. Option E summarizes part of the reactions of aerobic cellular respiration, which does provide energy for the reaction shown.

Question 86

Choice (D) is the correct answer. The individual with this genotype can produce two genetically different gametes for each gene. Since there are three genes, the number can be calculated by $2 \times 2 \times 2 = 8$, or the number can be derived by writing the possible combinations: *ABC*, *ABc*, *Abc*, *abc*, *aBC*, *abC*, *AbC*, and *aBc*.

Question 87

Choice (C) is the correct answer. In interphase, DNA is in long strands and is not observable as distinct chromosomes. The name for the collective strands is chromatin. Interphase is a nondividing phase of the cell life cycle. Option A describes metaphase of cell division. Option B describes the chromosomes during cell division. Option D describes the chromosomes in prophase I of meiosis. Option E is similar to tetrads; the terms are sometimes used interchangeably.

Question 88

Choice (A) is the correct answer. The rate of exchange of nutrients and water between a living cell and its environment depends mostly on the ratio of surface area to volume. A cell with a larger surface area relative to its volume can move more materials in and out at the same time. This is true of both eukaryotic and prokaryotic cells. The other options describe important characteristics of a cell, but they do not determine the rate of exchange.

Question 89

Choice (A) is the correct answer. Nondisjunction during meiosis results in some gametes having an extra chromosome (trisomy) and some gametes having one fewer chromosome (monosomy). In some cases, an individual can survive with either the extra or the missing chromosome, such as trisomy 21, also known as Down syndrome. Option B is incorrect, as the gametes will not be identical. Option C is incorrect, as the offspring produced from affected gametes will still be genetically different from the parents. Option D is incorrect for individuals with particular trisomies. Option E is incorrect, as the DNA will not change from linear to circular.

Question 90

Choice (C) is the correct answer. Option C could be blood type A or B: it is the only cross in which none of the offspring will be *ii*, which is the genotype for blood type O. Option A or E could result in offspring with blood type A or O, and option B or D could result in offspring with blood type B or O.

Question 91

Choice (D) is the correct answer. The graph shows two enzymes that have different reaction rates at different pH values. Enzyme X is active in more acidic conditions, with an optimal pH of 4. Enzyme Y is active over a broader pH range and has an optimal pH of 7. Both enzymes are active between pH 5 and pH 6, even though the rates of reaction are relatively low.

Question 92

Choice (B) is the correct answer. One of the primary functions of lipids is long-term energy storage in organisms. In animals, lipids are stored as fats, and in plants they are more often stored as oils. The other options give functions that are not associated with lipids.

Question 93

Choice (D) is the correct answer. The graph shows that the percent radioactivity is high initially in the endoplasmic reticulum (ER) and then drops. As the level drops in the ER, it rises and then falls in the Golgi apparatus. The level in the secretory granules increases throughout. This information is consistent with the synthesis of a protein that is being secreted out of the cell. Among options, only insulin is a secreted protein.

Question 94

Choice (B) is the correct answer. The data can be used to determine the path of a newly synthesized protein. The question that is best aligned with the data is given in option B. None of the other questions are relevant to the data.

Question 95

Choice (D) is the correct answer. Option D summarizes the secretory pathway: a protein is synthesized by the ribosomes on the rough endoplasmic reticulum, then transported to the Golgi apparatus for modification and packaging, and then secreted out of the cell by vesicles. This pathway is consistent with the data in the graph, whereas the pathways in the other options are not consistent (A and B) or refer to other macromolecules (C and E).

Question 96

Choice (C) is the correct answer. The number of bacteria present on day 12 is approximately 10^5, while the number present on day 4 is approximately 10^4. There are ten times as many bacterial cells on day 12 as on day 4.

Question 97

Choice (D) is the correct answer. Option D is the most reasonable conclusion. Option A is incorrect because the number of bacteria did not steadily decline through day 8. Option B is incorrect because streptomycin does not cause genetic mutations conferring resistance. Option C is incorrect because an alternate antibiotic might be effective; there is no evidence to suggest that it will be ineffective. Option E is incorrect because urine is sterile; it does not normally contain any bacteria.

Question 98

Choice (A) is the correct answer. The bag initially contained sugar, while the solution in the beaker did not. We are told that the membrane of the bag is selectively permeable, meaning that some material can pass through it. The most reasonable explanation for the presence of sugar in the beaker after 24 hours is diffusion. The sugar diffused from an area of high concentration (the bag) to an area with low concentration (the beaker) through the selectively permeable membrane. Options B and C require a living cell, and option D refers to osmosis, which is the movement of water, not solutes. Option D is absorption, which is not occurring here.

Question 99

Choice (E) is the correct answer. Starch, lipids, and proteins are generally very large molecules. Sugars are generally much smaller. The data suggest that the pore size of the dialysis membrane was large enough to let sugar pass but not the other, larger molecules. Options A, B, C, and D are not supported by the data presented.

Question 100

Choice (A) is the correct answer. The introductory material states that the volume of the bag increased during the 24-hour period, which supports statement I. There is no data to support statement II or statement III. Therefore, the correct answer is option A.

Biology E/M Subject Test - Practice Test 2

Practice Helps

The test that follows is an actual, previously administered SAT Subject Test in Biology E/M. To get an idea of what it's like to take this test, practice under conditions that are much like those of an actual test administration.

- Set aside an hour when you can take the test uninterrupted.

- Sit at a desk or table with no other books or papers. Dictionaries, other books, or notes are not allowed in the test room.

- Tear out an answer sheet from the back of this book and fill it in just as you would on the day of the test. One answer sheet can be used for up to three Subject Tests.

- Read the instructions that precede the practice test. During the actual administration you will be asked to read them before answering test questions.

- Time yourself by placing a clock or kitchen timer in front of you.

- After you finish the practice test, read the sections "How to Score the SAT Subject Test in Ecological Biology" or "How to Score the SAT Subject Test in Molecular Biology" and "How Did You Do on the Subject Test in Ecological Biology?" or "How Did You Do on the Subject Test in Molecular Biology?"

- The appearance of the answer sheet in this book may differ from the answer sheet you see on test day.

BIOLOGY–E TEST or BIOLOGY–M TEST

You must decide whether you want to take a Biology Test with Ecological Emphasis (BIOLOGY-E) or Molecular Emphasis (BIOLOGY-M) now, before the test begins. The top portion of the page of the answer sheet that you will use to take the Biology Test you have selected must be filled in exactly as illustrated below. When your supervisor tells you to fill in the circle next to the name of the test you are about to take, mark your answer sheet as shown.

For BIOLOGY-E

○ Literature	○ Mathematics Level 1	○ German	○ Chinese Listening	○ Japanese Listening
● Biology E	○ Mathematics Level 2	○ Italian	○ French Listening	○ Korean Listening
○ Biology M	○ U.S. History	○ Latin	○ German Listening	○ Spanish Listening
○ Chemistry	○ World History	○ Modern Hebrew		
○ Physics	○ French	○ Spanish	**Background Questions:** ① ② ③ ④ ⑤ ⑥ ⑦ ⑧ ⑨	

For BIOLOGY-M

○ Literature	○ Mathematics Level 1	○ German	○ Chinese Listening	○ Japanese Listening
○ Biology E	○ Mathematics Level 2	○ Italian	○ French Listening	○ Korean Listening
● Biology M	○ U.S. History	○ Latin	○ German Listening	○ Spanish Listening
○ Chemistry	○ World History	○ Modern Hebrew		
○ Physics	○ French	○ Spanish	**Background Questions:** ① ② ③ ④ ⑤ ⑥ ⑦ ⑧ ⑨	

After filling in the circle next to the name of the test you are taking, locate the Background Questions section, which also appears at the top of your answer sheet (as shown above). This is where you will answer the following Background Questions on your answer sheet.

BACKGROUND QUESTIONS

Please answer the four questions below by filling in the appropriate circle in the Background Questions box on your answer sheet. The information you provide is for statistical purposes only and will not affect your test score.

Question I   How many semesters of biology have you taken in high school? (If you are taking biology this semester, count it as a full semester.) Fill in only one circle of circles 1-3.

- One semester or less   — Fill in circle 1.
- Two semesters   — Fill in circle 2.
- Three semesters or more   — Fill in circle 3.

Question II   Which of the following best describes your biology course? Fill in only one circle of circles 4-6.

- General Biology   — Fill in circle 4.
- Biology with emphasis on ecology   — Fill in circle 5.
- Biology with emphasis on molecular biology   — Fill in circle 6.

Question III   Which of the following best describes your background in algebra? (If you are taking an algebra course this semester, count it as a full semester.) Fill in only one circle of circles 7-8.

- One semester or less   — Fill in circle 7.
- Two semesters or more   — Fill in circle 8.

Question IV   Have you had or are you currently taking Advanced Placement Biology? If you are, fill in circle 9.

When the supervisor gives the signal, turn the page and begin the Biology Test. There are 100 numbered circles on the answer sheet. There are 60 questions in the core Biology Test, 20 questions in the Biology-E section, and 20 questions in the Biology-M section. Therefore use ONLY circles 1-80 (for Biology-E) OR circles 1-60 plus 81-100 (for Biology-M) for recording your answers.

BIOLOGY E/M TEST

FOR BOTH BIOLOGY-E AND BIOLOGY-M,
ANSWER QUESTIONS 1-60

Directions: Each set of lettered choices below refers to the numbered questions or statements immediately following it. Select the one lettered choice that best answers each question or best fits each statement and then fill in the corresponding circle on the answer sheet. A choice may be used once, more than once, or not at all in each set.

Questions 1-4

(A) Mosses
(B) Ferns
(C) Gymnosperms
(D) Angiosperms
(E) Fungi

1. Organisms that do not carry out photosynthesis

2. Organisms that produce flowers

3. Photosynthetic organisms characterized by an absence of xylem and phloem

4. Multicellular organisms responsible for recycling nutrients into the soil

GO ON TO THE NEXT PAGE

Questions 5-8

The following illustrates several major regions of a typical root.

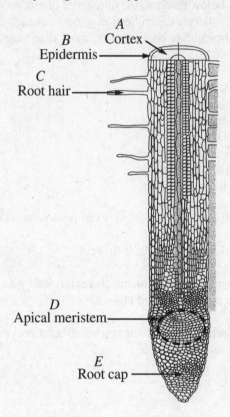

5. Portion of the root where the greatest frequency of mitosis occurs

6. Protects the meristem as the root elongates

7. Responsible for absorption of dissolved nutrients

8. Ground tissue surrounding the vascular tissue

Questions 9-11 refer to the following.

(A) Intron
(B) Allele
(C) Mutation
(D) Chromosome
(E) Chromatin

9. A change in DNA sequence

10. A noncoding segment of DNA

11. The primary source of new genetic variation

GO ON TO THE NEXT PAGE

Directions: Each of the questions or incomplete statements below is followed by five suggested answers or completions. Some questions pertain to a set that refers to a laboratory or experimental situation. For each question, select the one choice that is the best answer to the question and then fill in the corresponding circle on the answer sheet.

12. Which of the following statements about double-stranded DNA is true?

   (A) DNA always exists in a circular form.
   (B) The number of adenine nucleotides equals the number of uracil nucleotides in a double-stranded DNA molecule.
   (C) The number of guanine nucleotides equals the number of cytosine nucleotides in a double-stranded DNA molecule.
   (D) The sequences of nucleotides on both strands of a double-stranded DNA molecule are identical.
   (E) DNA is the genetic material in eukaryotes, but not in prokaryotes.

13. The first forms of life on Earth are hypothesized to have been heterotrophic prokaryotes. Many scientists think that those first cells were heterotrophs rather than autotrophs because

   (A) free oxygen was plentiful in the primitive atmosphere and therefore photosynthesis was unnecessary
   (B) there was so much water vapor in the atmosphere that sunlight could not penetrate
   (C) the early organic molecules were too acidic to support autotrophic cells
   (D) the evolution of heterotrophs would have involved fewer steps than would that of the more complex autotrophs
   (E) the high temperatures of early Earth inhibited photosynthetic activity

14. Bacteria that live in the root nodules of clover are most important in the continuation of the

   (A) carbon cycle
   (B) phosphorus cycle
   (C) water cycle
   (D) nitrogen cycle
   (E) sulfur cycle

15. The most common form of color blindness in humans is inherited as a sex-linked trait. If a man who is not color-blind and a woman who is not color-blind, but carries the allele for color blindness, have a son, what is the probability that this son will be color-blind?

   (A)   0%
   (B) 25%
   (C) 50%
   (D) 75%
   (E) 100%

16. Which of the following mammalian structures would be most likely to fossilize?

   (A) Cerebral cortex
   (B) Mammary glands
   (C) Kidney
   (D) Heart
   (E) Middle ear bones

17. Which of the following is an example of a Mendelian testcross to determine the genotype of an individual?

   (A) $AA \times Aa$
   (B) $Aa \times Aa$
   (C) $Aa \times aa$
   (D) $AaBB \times AaBB$
   (E) $AaBb \times AaBb$

18. Which of the following is most closely related to a mushroom?

   (A) An alga
   (B) A bacterium
   (C) A yeast
   (D) An oak tree
   (E) A moss

GO ON TO THE NEXT PAGE

19. Characteristics of tropical rain forests include all of the following EXCEPT

(A) extreme temperature fluctuations
(B) high humidity
(C) diverse animal life
(D) nutrient-poor soils
(E) a great variety of tall trees

20. Which of the following is true of oxygen?

(A) Oxygen gas has always been a major component of the Earth's atmosphere.
(B) Oxygen is highly reactive, but is nonetheless required for human survival.
(C) Oxygen is carried through the human bloodstream by aerobic bacteria with which humans have a symbiotic relationship.
(D) *E. coli* bacteria in the human small intestine convert lactose into oxygen gas, which is the basis of lactose intolerance.
(E) The energy released during cellular respiration comes from the reaction between oxygen and water.

21. Of the following, the determining factor in natural selection is the number of individuals that

(A) survive
(B) are produced
(C) migrate
(D) reproduce
(E) mutate

22. Which of the following best describes what is meant by the term "diploid"?

(A) Containing double-stranded DNA
(B) Containing only one copy of each chromosome
(C) Containing pairs of structurally similar chromosomes
(D) Containing pairs of chromosomes with identical DNA sequences
(E) Containing haphazardly arranged genes

23. Which of the following best describes the behavior displayed by domestic cats that run into the kitchen on hearing the sound of a can opener?

(A) Habituation
(B) Imprinting
(C) Problem-solving
(D) Conditioning
(E) Instinct

24. The structure found in human males that functions in both urinary and reproductive systems is the

(A) urethra
(B) fallopian tube
(C) vas deferens
(D) epididymis
(E) seminal vesicle

25. Some insect species resemble other insect species that are poisonous or distasteful. This resemblance is an example of

(A) mutation
(B) transformation
(C) inbreeding
(D) mimicry
(E) homology

26. In ruminant animals such as cows, bacteria inhabit the digestive tract and aid in the digestion of grasses. In this situation, the relationship between the bacteria and the cow is an example of

(A) parasitism
(B) saprophytism
(C) competition
(D) mutualism
(E) predation

27. Villi of the small intestine and alveoli of the lung are alike in all of the following ways EXCEPT:

(A) They increase the surface area for exchange of materials.
(B) They have a thin layer of epithelial tissue.
(C) They have extensive blood vessels.
(D) They are extremely numerous.
(E) They secrete a high volume of enzymes.

GO ON TO THE NEXT PAGE

28. Which of the following statements about temperature regulation in humans living in hot environments is correct?

   (A) Perspiration insulates the body and prevents heat loss.
   (B) Evaporation of perspiration cools the surface of the skin.
   (C) Blood is shunted from the head region to the body cavity.
   (D) Blood is more likely to travel near the long bones than near the skin.
   (E) Goose bumps cool by decreasing the surface area of the skin.

29. Which of the following could explain the fact that a woman whose ovulation is normal may be infertile?

   I. Her fallopian tubes are blocked.
   II. Large quantities of luteinizing hormone, LH, are released just prior to ovulation.
   III. Sperm movement is inhibited by an incompatible pH in the fluids of the vagina or uterus.

   (A) I only
   (B) II only
   (C) I and III only
   (D) II and III only
   (E) I, II, and III

30. The model for evolutionary change in which long periods of species stability are interrupted by brief periods of rapid change is

   (A) genetic isolation
   (B) Hardy-Weinberg equilibrium
   (C) acquired characteristics theory
   (D) punctuated equilibrium
   (E) gradualism

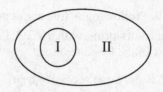

31. If the diagram above illustrates a relationship between existing taxonomic groups, which of the following is best illustrated by the diagram?

	Group I	Group II
(A)	Species	Species
(B)	Species	Genus
(C)	Genus	Species
(D)	Order	Genus
(E)	Phylum	Class

32. Which of the following best represents a food chain?

   (A) Seeds → mouse → snake → coyote → fleas
   (B) Mouse → snake → coyote → fleas → seeds
   (C) Seeds → fleas → mouse → coyote → snake
   (D) Fleas → mouse → coyote → seeds → snake
   (E) Snake → coyote → fleas → mouse → seeds

33. In the mammalian eye, the iris has which of the following functions?

   (A) It monitors impulse transmission along the auditory nerve.
   (B) It contains the rod and cone cells.
   (C) It regulates the size of the pupil opening.
   (D) It transmits images to the retina.
   (E) It provides lubrication for the cornea.

34. Nondisjunction of the sex chromosomes in a human female can result in her daughter inheriting a condition represented by

   (A) Y
   (B) YY
   (C) XY
   (D) XYY
   (E) XXX

GO ON TO THE NEXT PAGE

35. Which of the following is true about an F_1 cross that produces offspring with a 9:3:3:1 ratio of phenotypes in the F_2 generation?

   (A) There is only one recessive trait.
   (B) The genes involved are linked.
   (C) Three genes must be involved.
   (D) It represents a dihybrid cross.
   (E) Each phenotype is due to a single allele.

36. Many years ago a group of islands off the coast of South America were colonized by a single species of finch from the mainland. Each island now is inhabited by a different species of finch, all of which are descendants of the original colonizing species. This is an example of

   (A) convergent evolution
   (B) adaptive radiation
   (C) symbiosis
   (D) succession
   (E) continental drift

37. Crossing-over has a significant impact on which of the following?

   (A) Genetic variation
   (B) Formation of spindle fibers
   (C) Position of the kinetochore
   (D) Production of diploid cells
   (E) Age of the chromosome

38. The highest net primary productivity per unit area is found in which of the following biomes?

   (A) Estuaries
   (B) Coniferous forests
   (C) Deserts
   (D) Tundras
   (E) Grasslands

39. During a muscle contraction, the proteins actin and myosin slide along each other to decrease the length of the myofibril. Which of the following molecules directly allows for the movement of myosin relative to actin?

   (A) Glucose
   (B) ATP
   (C) NADH
   (D) ADP
   (E) NAD⁺

40. Which of the following pairs of organelles are capable of ATP production?

   (A) Ribosomes and mitochondria
   (B) Peroxisomes and food vacuoles
   (C) Microtubules and membranes
   (D) Mitochondria and chloroplasts
   (E) Lysosomes and Golgi bodies

41. One effect of increasing the concentration of antidiuretic hormone (ADH) is to

   (A) reduce the permeability to water in the loop of Henle
   (B) reduce the permeability to water of the collecting ducts
   (C) reduce the blood volume
   (D) increase the volume and output of urine
   (E) increase the concentration and decrease the volume of urine

42. Increasing the number of stomata on the upper surface of a leaf would most likely

   (A) increase evaporation of water from the leaf
   (B) cause more stomata on the under surface of the leaf to open
   (C) increase the rate of respiration
   (D) reduce transpiration
   (E) prevent the leaves from dropping off in the autumn

43. Which of the following is true of the trophic levels in an energy pyramid?

   (A) Only about 10% of the energy from one level is transferred to the next.
   (B) A given organism can only occupy one trophic level.
   (C) Consumers store more energy than producers.
   (D) Detritivores produce the energy for organisms at higher trophic levels.
   (E) Tertiary-level consumers are more numerous than producers and are likely to use more energy.

GO ON TO THE NEXT PAGE

Questions 44-46

The diagram below shows the size of the deer population in a particular ecosystem from 1905 to 1940. Between 1910 and 1920, hunters killed 3,000 coyotes, 600 mountain lions, and 11 wolves in that ecosystem.

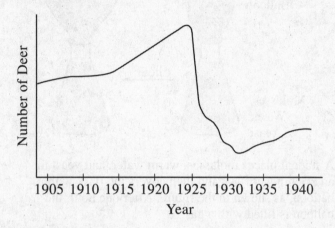

44. Predators apparently kept this deer herd near the carrying capacity during which of the following periods?

    (A) 1905–1910
    (B) 1920–1925
    (C) 1925–1930
    (D) 1930–1935
    (E) 1935–1940

45. All of the following could be a reasonable explanation for the significant decrease in the deer population after 1925 EXCEPT

    (A) overgrazing by the deer
    (B) resumption of the hunting of predators by humans
    (C) fires
    (D) a disease epidemic
    (E) the appearance of a new competitor

46. For this ecosystem, which of the following is best illustrated by the study?

    (A) Predators are harmful to the ecological balance.
    (B) Overgrazing by deer can control populations of weeds.
    (C) Severe winters destroy many animals.
    (D) The size of the deer population is dependent on predators and population density.
    (E) In the absence of predators, the deer population will increase indefinitely.

GO ON TO THE NEXT PAGE

Questions 47-51

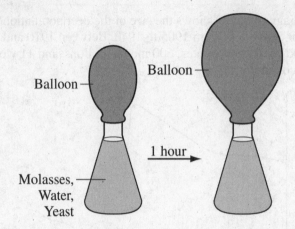

Balloon

Balloon

1 hour

Molasses,
Water,
Yeast

A student places molasses, warm water, and yeast in
an Erlenmeyer flask and then covers the flask with a
balloon, as shown in the figure. After one hour, the
balloon is filled with a gas.

47. The gas in the balloon is most likely

(A) oxygen
(B) methane
(C) helium
(D) carbon monoxide
(E) carbon dioxide

48. Which of the following is found in the molasses
and is most likely used by the yeast for energy?

(A) Sucrose
(B) Cellulose
(C) Amino acids
(D) Nucleotides
(E) Starch

49. If the flask had been cooled to 50°F (12°C), which
of the following predictions is most reasonable?

(A) No gas would have formed.
(B) The gas would have formed more slowly.
(C) The gas would have formed faster.
(D) A different gas would have formed.
(E) A mixture of gases would have formed.

50. Which of the following directly resulted in the
production of the gas?

(A) Carbohydrate synthesis
(B) Protein digestion
(C) Photosynthesis
(D) Chemiosmosis
(E) Fermentation

51. Which of the following would be the most likely
result if the yeast had been boiled before being
added to the flask?

(A) No gas would have formed.
(B) The gas would have formed more slowly.
(C) The gas would have formed faster.
(D) A different gas would have formed.
(E) A mixture of gases would have formed.

GO ON TO THE NEXT PAGE

Questions 52-56

DNA polymerase was isolated from a species of alga, from human cells, and from a species of bacterium found in a hot spring. The enzymatic reaction was measured at various temperatures for each species' enzyme. The results are shown on the graph below.

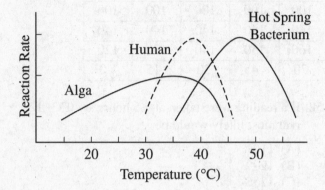

52. At which of the following temperatures does the human DNA polymerase show the greatest rate of activity?

(A) 25°C
(B) 28°C
(C) 30°C
(D) 37°C
(E) 46°C

53. Which of the following best explains the observation that the algal DNA polymerase increases in activity between 15°C and 30°C ?

(A) Enzyme reactions are temperature-dependent.
(B) Chemical reactions can be catalyzed by enzymes.
(C) Chemical reactions can occur in the absence of enzymes.
(D) Enzymes are not used up during the reactions they catalyze.
(E) Enzymes often require cofactors.

54. Which of the following best explains the observation that each enzyme shows a decline in activity at higher temperatures?

(A) Enzymes work best at room temperature.
(B) An enzyme may denature at high temperature.
(C) Enzyme structure is determined by the amino acid sequence.
(D) Enzymes unfold at low temperatures.
(E) The amino acids disintegrate.

55. Which of the following could explain the broad temperature range of the algal enzyme reaction, compared to the narrower range of the human enzyme reaction?

(A) Algae carry out photosynthesis, which raises their temperature.
(B) There are more species of algae than of humans.
(C) Algae and humans belong to different kingdoms.
(D) Humans live indoors, where temperature is regulated.
(E) Humans regulate their body temperature, while algae do not.

56. Which of the following is a reasonable prediction based on the data given for the study?

(A) The mitochondrial genes of the human and the bacterium are the same.
(B) The enzymes carry out different chemical reactions.
(C) The different species use different base-pairing rules in their DNA.
(D) The amino acid sequences of the three enzymes are not the same.
(E) The enzymes carry out their functions in the cytoplasm of cells.

GO ON TO THE NEXT PAGE

Questions 57-60

Observations of the respiration rate of pea seedlings at different temperatures over time produced the following data. The rates are given as a percentage of the rate at 25°C.

Temperature	0 hr	1 hr	2 hr	3 hr	4 hr	5 hr	6 hr	7 hr	8 hr
0°C	100	60	40	10	10	10	10	10	10
10°C	100	75	60	40	40	40	40	40	40
25°C	100	100	100	100	100	100	100	100	100
30°C	100	110	130	140	140	140	140	140	140
40°C	100	130	140	170	160	150	140	130	120
50°C	100	98	96	94	70	45	30	15	0

57. If the rate at 30°C is plotted against time, a graph of the results would look like which of the following?

(A)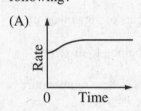

(B)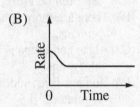

(C)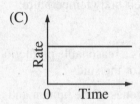

(D)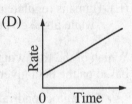

(E)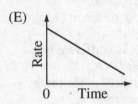

58. If a reading were taken at 7.5 hours at 40°C, the rate most likely would be

(A) 110%
(B) 120%
(C) 125%
(D) 130%
(E) 135%

59. The control temperature in the experiment is

(A) 0°C
(B) 10°C
(C) 25°C
(D) 30°C
(E) 50°C

60. According to the data, a pea seedling is most likely to die in 8 hours at which of the following temperatures?

(A) 0°C
(B) 10°C
(C) 25°C
(D) 40°C
(E) 50°C

If you are taking the Biology-E test, continue with questions 61-80.
If you are taking the Biology-M test, go to question 81 now.

GO ON TO THE NEXT PAGE

BIOLOGY-E SECTION

Directions: Each set of lettered choices below refers to the numbered questions or statements immediately following it. Select the one lettered choice that best answers each question or best fits each statement and then fill in the corresponding circle on the answer sheet. A choice may be used once, more than once, or not at all in each set.

Questions 61-63

(A) Decomposers
(B) Producers
(C) Primary consumers
(D) Secondary consumers
(E) Tertiary consumers

61. Organisms whose growth is directly limited by light intensity and nitrate availability

62. Rabbits that eat lettuce in a garden

63. Fish that feed on small herbivorous snails in a pond

GO ON TO THE NEXT PAGE

Directions: Each of the questions or incomplete statements below is followed by five suggested answers or completions. Some questions pertain to a set that refers to a laboratory or experimental situation. For each question, select the one choice that is the best answer to the question and then fill in the corresponding circle on the answer sheet.

64. Which of the following organisms maintains constant body temperature metabolically?

(A) Rattlesnake
(B) Salamander
(C) Lizard
(D) Ostrich
(E) Trout

65. Based on ecological principles, the planet Earth could support the largest number of people if they ate primarily

(A) cereals, fruit, and vegetables
(B) beef, pork, and lamb
(C) milk and milk products
(D) fish
(E) poultry

66. Which of the following is the best example of a population?

(A) A grouping of Douglas fir trees (*Pseudotsuga menziesii*) along the left bank of a Canadian river
(B) The sum of all the toads of the species *Bufo bufo* found in North America
(C) All the garter snakes of the subspecies *Thamnophis sirtalis sirtalis*
(D) The living organisms inhabiting a wooded area in central Maryland in 2001
(E) The organisms common to the chaparral

67. Which of the following organisms do NOT belong to the kingdom Plantae?

(A) Coniferous trees
(B) Fungi
(C) Angiosperms
(D) Mosses
(E) Liverworts

68. Numerous strains of mosquitoes now exist that can tolerate formerly lethal doses of the insecticide DDT. The most reasonable explanation for this decreased effectiveness of DDT is that

(A) the mosquitoes produced antibodies to DDT
(B) mosquitoes that were resistant to DDT survived and reproduced
(C) DDT decays over time
(D) DDT failed to interfere with the synthesis of messenger RNA
(E) DDT enhanced larval development in the mosquitoes

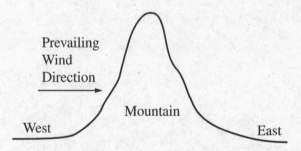

69. Along a mountain range in the western United States, as shown above, vegetation on the western slope differs significantly from that on the eastern slope in that vegetation on the western slope is

(A) sparser because of less available sunlight
(B) denser because of more available sunlight
(C) sparser because of less available moisture
(D) denser because of more available moisture
(E) sparser because of lower temperatures

GO ON TO THE NEXT PAGE

70. Some species have shown little evolutionary change for very long periods of time. The best explanation for the apparent lack of change is that the species

   (A) has been purged of harmful genes by inbreeding
   (B) is not capable of genetic variation
   (C) consists of members that are genetically homozygous recessive for many traits
   (D) has DNA that resists mutations
   (E) exists in an environmental niche that has remained relatively stable

71. Vitamins A, D, E, and K have which of the following in common?

   (A) They are not required in the human diet.
   (B) They are not components of visual pigments.
   (C) They are used in bone synthesis.
   (D) They are synthesized by humans.
   (E) They are fat soluble.

72. Which of the following pairs of characteristics best enables reptiles to thrive in desert ecosystems?

   (A) Glandular skin and hibernation
   (B) Cartilaginous endoskeleton and protective coloration
   (C) Four-chambered heart and endothermy
   (D) Advanced sensory systems and use of external fertilization
   (E) Keratinized skin and use of uric acid as an excretory product

73. Which of the following is NOT an example of energy flow through an ecosystem?

   (A) Energy from the Sun is converted to chemical energy in plants.
   (B) Decomposers break down dead organic material.
   (C) Usable nitrogen moves between organisms and the soil.
   (D) Some energy is lost as heat at each trophic level.
   (E) Consumers eat producers or other consumers.

74. In which of the following stages does a fern contain vascular tissue?

   (A) Spore
   (B) Sporophyte
   (C) Gamete
   (D) Gametophyte
   (E) Archegonium

75. Organisms inhabiting which of the following environments remove the least CO_2 from the atmosphere in the process of photosynthesis?

   (A) Tundra
   (B) Grassland
   (C) Deciduous forest
   (D) Tropical rain forest
   (E) Ocean

GO ON TO THE NEXT PAGE

Questions 76-77

THE MAJOR ZONES OF THE OCEAN

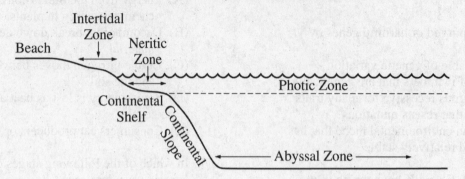

76. The LEAST amount of primary productivity occurs in which of the following?

(A) Abyssal zone
(B) Neritic zone
(C) Photic zone
(D) Continental shelf
(E) Continental slope

77. Adaptations necessary for survival of organisms in the abyssal zone include which of the following?

I. Tolerance of low temperature
II. Tolerance of high pressure
III. Requirement for high light intensity

(A) II only
(B) III only
(C) I and II only
(D) I and III only
(E) I, II, and III

GO ON TO THE NEXT PAGE

Questions 78-80

In a certain community of several species of annuals, plant I is always found attached to plant II by natural root grafts. Plant II specimens to which plant I is not attached are more vigorous. Ordinarily, the leaves of plant I are green, but some albino plants exist in the community. The albino plants flower and form seeds.

78. The fact that no specimen of plant I, even though green, is ever found growing independently suggests that

   (A) the vascular system for transporting food is defective in plant I
   (B) the roots of plant I are able to take up only water
   (C) plant I must be pollinated by plant II
   (D) plant I must make the environment suitable for plant II
   (E) plant I cannot produce a needed substance that it obtains from plant II

79. The observations that were made in this particular community suggest that

   (A) plant II would grow better in the absence of plant I
   (B) plant II would not be present if there were no plant I
   (C) plant II would attach to something else in the absence of plant I
   (D) plant I and plant II have formed a relationship from which both benefit
   (E) albinism will probably spread to plant II

80. Which of the following is the best inference about the albino plants?

   (A) Since they form seeds, photosynthesis occurs in the chloroplasts of their leaves, but the CO_2 comes from attached plant II.
   (B) The albinism is caused by an insufficient number of attachments to plant II.
   (C) The continued growth of the albino plants is evidence of the dependence of plant I on plant II.
   (D) Since a form of parasitism is involved, albinism in this case cannot be gene controlled.
   (E) The albinism is caused by the transduction of genes in plant II to plant I.

STOP
IF YOU FINISH BEFORE TIME IS CALLED, YOU MAY CHECK YOUR WORK ON THE ENTIRE BIOLOGY-E TEST.

If you are taking the Biology-M test, continue with questions 81-100.
Be sure to start this section of the test by filling in circle 81 on your answer sheet.

Directions: Each set of lettered choices below refers to the numbered questions or statements immediately following it. Select the one lettered choice that best answers each question or best fits each statement and then fill in the corresponding circle on the answer sheet. A choice may be used once, more than once, or not at all in each set.

Questions 81-84 refer to the following.

(A)

(B)

(C)

(D)

(E)

81. Molecule released upon hydrolysis of ATP

82. Molecule metabolized by glycolysis and aerobic respiration to produce ATP

83. Compound that is a basic structural unit of proteins

84. Composed of a nitrogenous base, a sugar, and a phosphate group

GO ON TO THE NEXT PAGE

Directions: Each of the questions or incomplete statements below is followed by five suggested answers or completions. Some questions pertain to a set that refers to a laboratory or experimental situation. For each question, select the one choice that is the best answer to the question and then fill in the corresponding circle on the answer sheet.

85. Which of the following is a substance that changes the rate of a reaction by lowering the energy of activation?

    (A) A hormone
    (B) A nucleotide
    (C) A cofactor
    (D) An enzyme
    (E) An antibody

86. Which of the following molecules is an initial reactant in glycolysis?

    (A) $NADP^+$

    (B) CO_2

    (C) $C_6H_{12}O_6$

    (D) ADP

    (E) O_2

87. All of the following cellular structures include membranes EXCEPT the

    (A) nucleolus
    (B) nuclear envelope
    (C) endoplasmic reticulum
    (D) mitochondrion
    (E) chloroplast

88. Which of the following is a common characteristic of all lipids?

    (A) They are acidic.
    (B) They are negatively charged.
    (C) They are hydrophobic.
    (D) They are made from amino acids.
    (E) They are phosphorylated.

89. In a man showing the recessive phenotype for a particular autosomal trait, what is the expected percentage of his sperm cells that will carry the recessive allele associated with this trait?

    (A)   0%
    (B) 25%
    (C) 50%
    (D) 75%
    (E) 100%

90. Prokaryotes differ from eukaryotes in that prokaryotes

    (A) have only a nucleus, cell membrane, and cytoplasm
    (B) have ribosomes and mitochondria
    (C) have a true nucleus and may have a cell wall
    (D) lack a true nucleus but may have a cell wall
    (E) lack DNA but can synthesize proteins

91. Restriction fragment length polymorphisms (RFLPs) are helpful in which of the following?

    (A) Determining antigen/antibody relationships
    (B) Establishing a baseline for blood-typing
    (C) Determining protein content
    (D) Determining DNA fingerprints
    (E) Determining the polymerase chain reaction (PCR) imprint

92. Which of the following is true of the Golgi apparatus?

    (A) It is especially extensive in cells specialized for absorption.
    (B) It consists of flattened membranes dotted with ribosomes.
    (C) It is a membrane-bound vesicle with hydrolytic enzymes.
    (D) It is specialized for production of hydrogen peroxide.
    (E) It is involved in modifying and shipping proteins out of cells.

GO ON TO THE NEXT PAGE

93. Which of the following is a characteristic of both mitochondria and chloroplasts?

(A) Presence of light-capturing pigments
(B) Production of CO_2
(C) Production of O_2 as a waste product
(D) The ability to synthesize glucose
(E) The ability to synthesize ATP

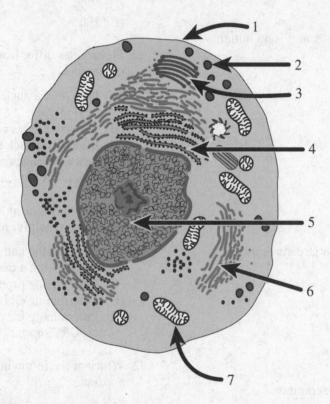

94. Using the labeled diagram shown above, which of the following correctly presents the pathway followed by a protein synthesized for secretion?

(A) 1, 2, 3
(B) 5, 6, 7
(C) 4, 3, 2
(D) 5, 3, 2
(E) 2, 3, 4

GO ON TO THE NEXT PAGE

95. Phospholipids are components of which of the following?

    (A) Chromatin
    (B) Ribosome
    (C) Cytoskeleton
    (D) Spindle apparatus
    (E) Cell membrane

96. An animal breeder notices that one breeding pair nearly always produces at least one albino per litter, with a ratio of 1 albino to 3 normally pigmented animals. All the albinos from this breeding pair are male. Which of the following is the most likely mode of inheritance for this type of albinism?

    (A) Autosomal recessive
    (B) Autosomal dominant
    (C) Autosomal lethal
    (D) Sex-linked dominant
    (E) Sex-linked recessive

97. Which of the following is a correct statement about both anaerobic cellular respiration and aerobic cellular respiration?

    (A) Both processes utilize amino acids as a primary fuel source.
    (B) In anaerobic cellular respiration, glycolysis takes place outside mitochondria; in aerobic cellular respiration, glycolysis takes place inside mitochondria.
    (C) Both processes produce ATP.
    (D) Anaerobic cellular respiration occurs only in prokaryotes; aerobic cellular respiration occurs only in eukaryotes.
    (E) Photons are required to initiate both processes.

GO ON TO THE NEXT PAGE

Questions 98-100

The following diagram depicts one way that certain retroviruses can cause cancer in animal cells.

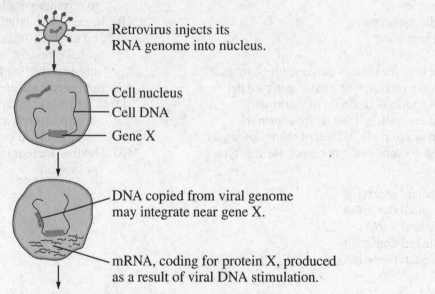

Retrovirus injects its RNA genome into nucleus.

Cell nucleus
Cell DNA
Gene X

DNA copied from viral genome may integrate near gene X.

mRNA, coding for protein X, produced as a result of viral DNA stimulation.

Cell divides rapidly, producing cancer cells, all containing viral genes.

98. Based on the diagram, what is the likely function of protein X?

(A) Initiating an immune response
(B) Initiating cell death
(C) Stimulating cell division
(D) Forming the viral coat protein
(E) Producing ATP

99. Which of the following characteristics is unique to retroviruses like the one described?

(A) They contain nucleic acids.
(B) They can infect both prokaryotic and eukaryotic cells.
(C) They contain proteins in their coats.
(D) They contain the code for reverse transcriptase enzymes.
(E) They mutate rapidly.

100. On the basis of the diagram, a logical conclusion about the relationship between viruses and cancer is that

(A) all viruses cause cancer
(B) viruses can change normal cells into cancer cells
(C) pollutants stimulate viruses to cause cancer
(D) cells do not become cancerous until they have been infected by many viruses
(E) viral RNA becomes attached to DNA in cancer cells

S T O P

IF YOU FINISH BEFORE TIME IS CALLED, YOU MAY CHECK YOUR WORK ON THE ENTIRE BIOLOGY-M TEST. DO NOT TURN TO ANY OTHER TEST IN THIS BOOK.

NO TEST MATERIAL ON THIS PAGE

How to Score the SAT Subject Test in Ecological Biology

When you take an actual SAT Subject Test in Ecological Biology, your answer sheet will be "read" by a scanning machine that will record your response to each question. Then a computer will compare your answers with the correct answers and produce your raw score. You get one point for each correct answer. For each wrong answer, you lose one-fourth of a point. Questions you omit (and any for which you mark more than one answer) are not counted. This raw score is converted to a scaled score that is reported to you and to the colleges you specify.

Worksheet 1. Finding Your Raw Test Score

STEP 1: Table A on the following page lists the correct answers for all the questions on the Subject Test in Ecological Biology that is reproduced in this book. It also serves as a worksheet for you to calculate your raw score.

- Compare your answers with those given in the table.

- Put a check in the column marked "Right" if your answer is correct.

- Put a check in the column marked "Wrong" if your answer is incorrect.

- Leave both columns blank if you omitted the question.

STEP 2: Count the number of right answers.

Enter the total here: _____

STEP 3: Count the number of wrong answers.

Enter the total here: _____

STEP 4: Multiply the number of wrong answers by .250.

Enter the product here: _____

STEP 5: Subtract the result obtained in Step 4 from the total you obtained in Step 2.

Enter the result here: _____

STEP 6: Round the number obtained in Step 5 to the nearest whole number.

Enter the result here: _____

The number you obtained in Step 6 is your raw score.

Answers to Practice Test 2 for Ecological Biology

Table A
Answers to the Subject Test in Ecological Biology - Practice Test 2 and Percentage of Students Answering Each Question Correctly

Question Number	Correct Answer	Right	Wrong	Percent Answering Correctly*	Question Number	Correct Answer	Right	Wrong	Percent Answering Correctly*
1	E			66	26	D			83
2	D			58	27	E			57
3	A			53	28	B			82
4	E			72	29	C			40
5	D			53	30	D			58
6	E			58	31	B			64
7	C			66	32	A			68
8	A			19	33	C			53
9	C			90	34	E			63
10	A			62	35	D			48
11	C			47	36	B			44
12	C			73	37	A			80
13	D			33	38	A			22
14	D			68	39	B			56
15	C			43	40	D			66
16	E			71	41	E			33
17	C			28	42	A			47
18	C			51	43	A			79
19	A			40	44	A			52
20	B			35	45	B			63
21	D			48	46	D			75
22	C			37	47	E			56
23	D			58	48	A			58
24	A			64	49	B			78
25	D			74	50	E			66

Table A continued on next page

Table A continued from previous page

Question Number	Correct Answer	Right	Wrong	Percent Answering Correctly*	Question Number	Correct Answer	Right	Wrong	Percent Answering Correctly*
51	A			53	66	A			47
52	D			91	67	B			67
53	A			73	68	B			79
54	B			81	69	D			35
55	E			71	70	E			83
56	D			43	71	E			25
57	A			92	72	E			31
58	C			84	73	C			50
59	C			81	74	B			18
60	E			93	75	A			48
61	B			78	76	A			73
62	C			89	77	C			86
63	D			87	78	E			74
64	D			65	79	A			76
65	A			74	80	C			46

* These percentages are based on an analysis of the answer sheets for a random sample of 3,334 students who took the original administration of this test and whose mean score was 592. They may be used as an indication of the relative difficulty of a particular question. Each percentage may also be used to predict the likelihood that a typical Subject Test in Ecological Biology candidate will answer correctly that question on this edition of this test.

Note: Answer explanations can be found on page 128.

Finding Your Scaled Score

When you take SAT Subject Tests, the scores sent to the colleges you specify are reported on the College Board scale, which ranges from 200-800. You can convert your practice test score to a scaled score by using Table B. To find your scaled score, locate your raw score in the left-hand column of Table B; the corresponding score in the right-hand column is your scaled score. For example, a raw score of 21 on this particular edition of the Subject Test in Ecological Biology corresponds to a scaled score of 470.

Raw scores are converted to scaled scores to ensure that a score earned on any one edition of a particular Subject Test is comparable to the same scaled score earned on any other edition of the same Subject Test. Because some editions of the tests may be slightly easier or more difficult than others, College Board scaled scores are adjusted so that they indicate the same level of performance regardless of the edition of the test taken and the ability of the group that takes it. Thus, for example, a score of 400 on one edition of a test taken at a particular administration indicates the same level of achievement as a score of 400 on a different edition of the test taken at a different administration.

When you take the SAT Subject Tests during a national administration, your scores are likely to differ somewhat from the scores you obtain on the tests in this book. People perform at different levels at different times for reasons unrelated to the tests themselves. The precision of any test is also limited because it represents only a sample of all the possible questions that could be asked.

Table B
Scaled Score Conversion Table
Subject Test in Ecological Biology - Practice Test 2

Raw Score	Scaled Score	Raw Score	Scaled Score	Raw Score	Scaled Score
80	800	40	580	0	320
79	800	39	580	−1	310
78	800	38	570	−2	300
77	800	37	560	−3	290
76	800	36	560	−4	290
75	790	35	550	−5	280
74	790	34	550	−6	270
73	780	33	540	−7	260
72	770	32	540	−8	250
71	770	31	530	−9	240
70	760	30	520	−10	230
69	750	29	520	−11	220
68	750	28	510	−12	220
67	740	27	510	−13	210
66	740	26	500	−14	200
65	730	25	500	−15	200
64	720	24	490	−16	200
63	720	23	480	−17	200
62	710	22	480	−18	200
61	700	21	470	−19	200
60	700	20	470	−20	200
59	690	19	460		
58	690	18	450		
57	680	17	450		
56	670	16	440		
55	670	15	430		
54	660	14	430		
53	660	13	420		
52	650	12	410		
51	650	11	410		
50	640	10	400		
49	630	9	390		
48	630	8	380		
47	620	7	380		
46	620	6	370		
45	610	5	360		
44	610	4	350		
43	600	3	340		
42	590	2	340		
41	590	1	330		

How Did You Do on the Subject Test in Ecological Biology?

After you score your test and analyze your performance, think about the following questions:

Did you run out of time before reaching the end of the test?

If so, you may need to pace yourself better. For example, maybe you spent too much time on one or two hard questions. A better approach might be to skip the ones you can't answer right away and try answering all the questions that remain on the test. Then if there's time, go back to the questions you skipped.

Did you take a long time reading the directions?

You will save time when you take the test by learning the directions to the Subject Test in Ecological Biology ahead of time. Each minute you spend reading directions during the test is a minute that you could use to answer questions.

How did you handle questions you were unsure of?

If you were able to eliminate one or more of the answer choices as wrong and guess from the remaining ones, your approach probably worked to your advantage. On the other hand, making haphazard guesses or omitting questions without trying to eliminate choices could cost you valuable points.

How difficult were the questions for you compared with other students who took the test?

Table A shows you how difficult the multiple-choice questions were for the group of students who took this test during its national administration. The right-hand column gives the percentage of students that answered each question correctly.

A question answered correctly by almost everyone in the group is obviously an easier question. For example, 83 percent of the students answered question 26 correctly. But only 25 percent answered question 71 correctly.

Keep in mind that these percentages are based on just one group of students. They would probably be different with another group of students taking the test.

If you missed several easier questions, go back and try to find out why: Did the questions cover material you haven't yet reviewed? Did you misunderstand the directions?

How to Score the SAT Subject Test in Molecular Biology

When you take an actual SAT Subject Test in Molecular Biology, your answer sheet will be "read" by a scanning machine that will record your response to each question. Then a computer will compare your answers with the correct answers and produce your raw score. You get one point for each correct answer. For each wrong answer, you lose one-fourth of a point. Questions you omit (and any for which you mark more than one answer) are not counted. This raw score is converted to a scaled score that is reported to you and to the colleges you specify.

Worksheet 1. Finding Your Raw Test Score

STEP 1: Table A on the following page lists the correct answers for all the questions on the Subject Test in Molecular Biology that is reproduced in this book. It also serves as a worksheet for you to calculate your raw score.

- Compare your answers with those given in the table.

- Put a check in the column marked "Right" if your answer is correct.

- Put a check in the column marked "Wrong" if your answer is incorrect.

- Leave both columns blank if you omitted the question.

STEP 2: Count the number of right answers.

Enter the total here: _____

STEP 3: Count the number of wrong answers.

Enter the total here: _____

STEP 4: Multiply the number of wrong answers by .250.

Enter the product here: _____

STEP 5: Subtract the result obtained in Step 4 from the total you obtained in Step 2.

Enter the result here: _____

STEP 6: Round the number obtained in Step 5 to the nearest whole number.

Enter the result here: _____

The number you obtained in Step 6 is your raw score.

Answers to Practice Test 2 for Molecular Biology

Table A
Answers to the Subject Test in Molecular Biology - Practice Test 2 and Percentage of Students Answering
Each Question Correctly

Question Number	Correct Answer	Right	Wrong	Percent Answering Correctly*	Question Number	Correct Answer	Right	Wrong	Percent Answering Correctly*
1	E			66	26	D			83
2	D			62	27	E			65
3	A			54	28	B			84
4	E			71	29	C			42
5	D			57	30	D			57
6	E			60	31	B			66
7	C			70	32	A			63
8	A			23	33	C			56
9	C			93	34	E			75
10	A			74	35	D			59
11	C			48	36	B			40
12	C			84	37	A			88
13	D			31	38	A			18
14	D			65	39	B			67
15	C			49	40	D			82
16	E			72	41	E			34
17	C			34	42	A			51
18	C			48	43	A			75
19	A			34	44	A			49
20	B			36	45	B			61
21	D			44	46	D			76
22	C			42	47	E			63
23	D			57	48	A			61
24	A			65	49	B			81
25	D			71	50	E			70

Table A continued on next page

Table A continued from previous page

Question Number	Correct Answer	Right	Wrong	Percent Answering Correctly*	Question Number	Correct Answer	Right	Wrong	Percent Answering Correctly*
51	A			58	86	C			71
52	D			92	87	A			44
53	A			78	88	C			77
54	B			88	89	E			51
55	E			70	90	D			75
56	D			49	91	D			22
57	A			94	92	E			84
58	C			85	93	E			81
59	C			85	94	C			55
60	E			97	95	E			86
81	A			61	96	E			69
82	E			62	97	C			75
83	C			66	98	C			71
84	B			89	99	D			44
85	D			83	100	B			82

* These percentages are based on an analysis of the answer sheets for a random sample of 4,402 students who took the original administration of this test and whose mean score was 605. They may be used as an indication of the relative difficulty of a particular question. Each percentage may also be used to predict the likelihood that a typical Subject Test in Molecular Biology candidate will answer correctly that question on this edition of this test.

Note: Answer explanations can be found on page 128.

Finding Your Scaled Score

When you take SAT Subject Tests, the scores sent to the colleges you specify are reported on the College Board scale, which ranges from 200-800. You can convert your practice test score to a scaled score by using Table B. To find your scaled score, locate your raw score in the left-hand column of Table B; the corresponding score in the right-hand column is your scaled score. For example, a raw score of 21 on this particular edition of the Subject Test in Molecular Biology corresponds to a scaled score of 470.

Raw scores are converted to scaled scores to ensure that a score earned on any one edition of a particular Subject Test is comparable to the same scaled score earned on any other edition of the same Subject Test. Because some editions of the tests may be slightly easier or more difficult than others, College Board scaled scores are adjusted so that they indicate the same level of performance regardless of the edition of the test taken and the ability of the group that takes it. Thus, for example, a score of 400 on one edition of a test taken at a particular administration indicates the same level of achievement as a score of 400 on a different edition of the test taken at a different administration.

When you take the SAT Subject Tests during a national administration, your scores are likely to differ somewhat from the scores you obtain on the tests in this book. People perform at different levels at different times for reasons unrelated to the tests themselves. The precision of any test is also limited because it represents only a sample of all the possible questions that could be asked.

Table B
Scaled Score Conversion Table
Subject Test in Molecular Biology - Practice Test 2

Raw Score	Scaled Score	Raw Score	Scaled Score	Raw Score	Scaled Score
80	800	40	580	0	320
79	800	39	570	−1	310
78	800	38	570	−2	310
77	790	37	560	−3	300
76	790	36	550	−4	290
75	780	35	550	−5	290
74	780	34	540	−6	280
73	770	33	540	−7	270
72	760	32	530	−8	260
71	760	31	530	−9	260
70	750	30	520	−10	250
69	740	29	520	−11	240
68	740	28	510	−12	230
67	730	27	500	−13	220
66	720	26	500	−14	220
65	720	25	490	−15	210
64	710	24	490	−16	210
63	700	23	480	−17	200
62	700	22	480	−18	200
61	690	21	470	−19	200
60	690	20	470	−20	200
59	680	19	460		
58	680	18	450		
57	670	17	450		
56	660	16	440		
55	660	15	430		
54	650	14	430		
53	650	13	420		
52	640	12	410		
51	640	11	410		
50	630	10	400		
49	630	9	390		
48	620	8	380		
47	620	7	380		
46	610	6	370		
45	600	5	360		
44	600	4	350		
43	590	3	350		
42	590	2	340		
41	580	1	330		

How Did You Do on the Subject Test in Molecular Biology?

After you score your test and analyze your performance, think about the following questions:

Did you run out of time before reaching the end of the test?

If so, you may need to pace yourself better. For example, maybe you spent too much time on one or two hard questions. A better approach might be to skip the ones you can't answer right away and try answering all the questions that remain on the test. Then if there's time, go back to the questions you skipped.

Did you take a long time reading the directions?

You will save time when you take the test by learning the directions to the Subject Test in Molecular Biology ahead of time. Each minute you spend reading directions during the test is a minute that you could use to answer questions.

How did you handle questions you were unsure of?

If you were able to eliminate one or more of the answer choices as wrong and guess from the remaining ones, your approach probably worked to your advantage. On the other hand, making haphazard guesses or omitting questions without trying to eliminate choices could cost you valuable points.

How difficult were the questions for you compared with other students who took the test?

Table A shows you how difficult the multiple-choice questions were for the group of students who took this test during its national administration. The right-hand column gives the percentage of students that answered each question correctly.

A question answered correctly by almost everyone in the group is obviously an easier question. For example, 83 percent of the students answered question 26 correctly. But only 22 percent answered question 91 correctly.

Keep in mind that these percentages are based on just one group of students. They would probably be different with another group of students taking the test.

If you missed several easier questions, go back and try to find out why: Did the questions cover material you haven't yet reviewed? Did you misunderstand the directions?

Answer Explanations

For Practice Test 2

Question 1

Choice (E) is the correct answer. Of the groups of organisms listed, only fungi do <u>not</u> carry out photosynthesis. Mosses (A), ferns (B), gymnosperms (C), and angiosperms (D) are all photosynthetic.

Question 2

Choice (D) is the correct answer. The angiosperms, which are commonly known as the flowering plants, are the groups of plants that produce flowers for reproduction. Mosses (A), ferns (B), gymnosperms (C) and fungi (E) all reproduce without flowers.

Question 3

Choice (A) is the correct answer. Xylem and phloem are types of vascular tissue found in the groups of plants termed vascular plants. The question asks about photosynthetic organisms, so fungi (E) are ruled out. Mosses (A), ferns (B), gymnosperms (C), and angiosperms (D) are all photosynthetic, and of these, only mosses lack vascular tissue consisting of xylem and phloem.

Question 4

Choice (E) is the correct answer. Fungi are the multicellular organisms that recycle nutrients into the soil. (Note that bacteria also recycle nutrients, but they are not multicellular.)

Question 5

Choice (D) is the correct answer. In a plant root, the greatest frequency of mitosis (cell division) occurs at point D, the apical meristem.

Question 6

Choice (E) is the correct answer. The root cap (E) is the structure that protects the growing root. It covers the apical meristem, where mitosis occurs, and offers protection to the growing root tip.

Question 7

Choice (C) is the correct answer. Root hairs (C) are the structures responsible for the absorption of dissolved nutrients. They provide a large surface area for the root to absorb water and dissolved nutrients.

Question 8

Choice (A) is the correct answer. The cortex surrounding the vascular tissue in the root is considered ground tissue, a term that refers to nonvascular, nondermal structures that function in support and storage.

Question 9

Choice (C) is the correct answer. A change in an established DNA nucleotide sequence is a mutation. There are many different types of mutation. Mutations may result in different alleles of a gene (B), but alleles do not cause a change in DNA sequence.

Question 10

Choice (A) is the correct answer. A noncoding segment of DNA is an intron. In eukaryotes, introns are generally removed during the production of mRNA. The term intron can refer to both the noncoding segment in the DNA and to the corresponding sequence in an RNA transcript. Chromosomes (D) and chromatin (E) typically contain many genes and therefore possess both coding and noncoding sequences.

Question 11

Choice (C) is the correct answer. Mutations are the primary source of new genetic variation. A change in the DNA sequence can result in a different allele of a gene that affects a particular trait and leads to variation in that trait within the population.

Question 12

Choice (C) is the correct answer. Double-stranded DNA consists of two complementary strands of DNA. Of the four nucleotides present in DNA, adenine on one strand of DNA forms hydrogen bonds with thymine on the other strand, and cytosine on one strand of DNA forms hydrogen bonds with guanine on the other strand. Therefore, a DNA molecule with a certain number of guanine nucleotides will have the same number of cytosine nucleotides. Option A is incorrect because DNA is not always circular; it is linear in eukaryotes. Option B is incorrect because uracil is found in RNA, not in DNA. Option D is incorrect because the sequences are not identical; they are complementary. Option E is incorrect because the primary genetic material of both eukaryotes and prokaryotes is DNA.

Question 13

Choice (D) is the correct answer. Since all organisms undergo cellular respiration, it is assumed that respiration evolved before photosynthesis. Autotrophs, organisms that undergo both cellular respiration and photosynthesis, require an additional and very complicated process that evolved later. Option A is incorrect because free oxygen was not plentiful in the early atmosphere of Earth. Option B is incorrect because sunlight could penetrate the atmosphere of early Earth. Option C is incorrect because the acidity of the early molecules is not related to the support of autotrophic cells. Option E is incorrect because on early Earth, while the temperatures were likely high, photosynthesis had not yet evolved and so was not inhibited.

Question 14

Choice (D) is the correct answer. The bacteria living in the root nodules of clover are nitrogen-fixing bacteria. They commonly are in association with plants called legumes. Through this symbiotic relationship, the plants obtain nitrogen in a form they can use. Atmospheric nitrogen (N_2) is not usable by plants but can be converted to usable nitrogen by the bacteria. The other nutrient cycles listed are not specific to root nodules.

Question 15

Choice (C) is the correct answer. In this instance, the sex-linked trait is associated with a gene that is carried on the X chromosome. Males have one X chromosome and one Y chromosome. Females have two X chromosomes. A son can only inherit the Y chromosome from his father and an X chromosome from his mother. He has an equal probability of inheriting either of the two X chromosomes from his mother. Since the mother carries the allele for color blindness on one of the X chromosomes, the son has a 50 percent chance of inheriting the allele and thus a 50 percent chance of being color-blind.

Question 16

Choice (E) is the correct answer. Fossilization is more likely to occur on harder structures, such as bones and teeth. Of the options, A, B, C, and D are soft tissues, which are less likely to fossilize.

Question 17

Choice (C) is the correct answer. A testcross is one in which an individual displaying a dominant phenotype for a particular trait is crossed with a known homozygous recessive individual. From this parent, all offspring inherit one recessive allele. If the offspring include individuals that display the recessive trait, then the parent with the dominant phenotype must have contributed a recessive allele to the offspring and is therefore a heterozygote. Of the options, only C includes one parent that is homozygous recessive.

Question 18

Choice (C) is the correct answer. A yeast is a type of fungus, as is a mushroom. An alga (A) is a protist, a bacterium (B) is a prokaryote, and an oak tree (D) and a moss (E) are both plants.

Question 19

Choice (A) is the correct answer. Note that this is a negative stem. Tropical rain forests are characterized by high humidity (B), high species diversity (C), nutrient-poor soils (D), and a variety of tree species making up the canopy (E). Option A, extreme temperature fluctuations, is <u>not</u> a characteristic of a tropical rain forest.

Question 20

Choice (B) is the correct answer. Oxygen is reactive and is necessary for the survival of humans and many other organisms on Earth as it can participate in a number of oxidation reactions in cells. Option A is incorrect because oxygen was not present in the atmosphere of early Earth. Option C is incorrect because bacteria do not assist with the transport of oxygen in the human body. Option D is incorrect because the bacteria do not convert lactose into oxygen gas. Option E is incorrect because the energy released during cellular respiration comes from many reactions involved in the breakdown of glucose, not from the simple interaction of oxygen and water.

Question 21

Choice (D) is the correct answer. A trait is only passed on to the next generation if there is successful reproduction by the individual with the trait. Options A, B, C, and D do not include passing on the trait.

Question 22

Choice (C) is the correct answer. When there are two chromosomes for each pair of chromosomes, the cell is diploid, which is represented as "2n." A haploid cell, such as a gamete, has one chromosome from each pair (B) and is represented as "n." Each chromosome in a pair is inherited from the one of the parents, so they are not identical (D). The DNA in the chromosomes is always double-stranded (A); this does not describe the ploidy. Arrangement of genes (E) does not describe ploidy.

Question 23

Choice (D) is the correct answer. In this case, the cats have learned that the sound of the can opener means they are likely to be fed; in other words, they are conditioned to the outcome of the sound. Option A is incorrect because habituation is a different type of learned behavior—getting accustomed to something, such as a recurring noise. Options B is incorrect because imprinting is a special case of programmed learning that occurs at a specific time during an animal's development. Option C is incorrect because the cats are not solving a problem. Option E is incorrect because instinct is a type of innate or genetically programmed behavior.

Question 24

Choice (A) is the correct answer. In males, the urethra can carry urine or seminal fluid. Fallopian tubes (B) are part of the female reproductive tract (these are termed the oviducts in nonhuman mammals). The structures in C, D, and E are all found in human males and function in the reproductive system, but they do not play a role in the urinary system.

Question 25

Choice (D) is the correct answer. An insect that resembles a poisonous or distasteful insect, such as a hover fly resembling a distasteful wasp, can avoid predation by mimicking the distasteful insect. Option A is incorrect because mutation is a change in DNA. Option B is incorrect because transformation is when a cell takes up a piece of foreign DNA into. Option C is incorrect because inbreeding is within a single species. Option E is incorrect because homology is the similarity of structures due to common ancestry.

Question 26

Choice (D) is the correct answer. Mutualism is a symbiotic relationship in which both individuals benefit. The bacteria gain access to nutrients, and the cow's digestion of the grasses is expedited. Option A and E are incorrect because parasitism and predation are relationships in which one organism benefits and the other does not. Option B is incorrect because saprophytism is feeding on dead or decaying matter. Option C is incorrect because the bacteria and the cow are not competing for resources.

Question 27

Choice (E) is the correct answer. Note that this question has a negative stem. Villi of the small intestine and alveoli of the lung both have increased surface area for exchange of materials (A); have thin layers of epithelial tissue (B); have networks of blood vessels (C), generally capillaries; and are numerous (D), to aid in the exchange of materials across membranes. The alveoli do not secrete high volumes of enzymes (E), while the villi of the small intestine do secrete enzymes involved in digestion.

Question 28

Choice (B) is the correct answer. The evaporation of perspiration or sweat has a cooling effect on the surface of the skin. Option A is incorrect because perspiration does not insulate the body. Options C and D describe incorrect blood flow. Option E is incorrect because goose bumps tend to form when a person is cold. They do not have a cooling function.

Question 29

Choice (C) is the correct answer. Blocked fallopian tubes can prevent conception. Incompatible pH in the vagina or uterus can also prevent conception. Luteinizing hormone (LH) triggers ovulation. We are told the woman has normal ovulation, so the problem in conceiving occurs after ovulation and does not result from the release of LH.

Question 30

Choice (D) is the correct answer. Punctuated equilibrium is the model of evolution in which there are long periods when species are stable and then there are short periods of rapid change. Genetic isolation (A) is one possible mechanism of speciation. The Hardy-Weinberg equilibrium (B) is a model of population genetics. The acquired characteristics theory, as put forth by Lamarck, (C) is not accepted as a model of evolution. Gradualism (E) states that evolution occurs slowly over a long period of time.

Question 31

Choice (B) is the correct answer. The diagram shows a smaller unit (I) contained within a larger unit (II). Of the options, the only one in which group I is a subset of group II is B: species are a subset of genus.

Question 32

Choice (A) is the correct answer. The arrows in a food chain represent the flow of energy and matter through the system. The only option that lists a correct flow of energy is option A. Fleas in a food chain consume blood from the coyote, which eats snakes, which eat mice, which eat seeds. Seeds cannot consume other organisms (B, D, and E), fleas do not consume seeds, nor do snakes consume coyotes (C).

Question 33

Choice (C) is the correct answer. The iris regulates the size of the pupil and thus regulates the amount of light that reaches the retina. The other functions listed are associated with different structures, not the iris.

Question 34

Choice (E) is the correct answer. Nondisjunction is the process in which the chromosomes in a homologous pair do not separate properly during meiosis, producing gametes with either an extra chromosome or a missing chromosome. Since females have two X chromosomes, this female would produce otherwise haploid gametes with two X chromosomes (XX) or no X chromosome (O). Since the child is a daughter, all of options with Y chromosomes can be ruled out. The gamete from the father would contain a single X chromosome. The daughter could be XO (not a choice here) or XXX (option E).

Question 35

Choice (D) is the correct answer. The 9:3:3:1 ratio is the predicted phenotypic ratio of the F_2 offspring from a dihybrid cross in which both traits are determined by dominant or recessive alleles. The parental generation is homozygous for both traits and the F_1 generation shows the dominant phenotype for both traits, but all individuals in the F_1 are heterozygous for both traits.

Question 36

Choice (B) is the correct answer. The scenario described is best explained by adaptive radiation. Option A is incorrect because convergent evolution is exemplified by unrelated organisms that have similar adaptations to their environment, such as the body shape of a porpoise and a shark. Option C is incorrect because symbiosis describes a relationship between two organisms. Option D is incorrect because succession is an ecological process involving a pattern of change in the organisms in an environment over time. Option E is incorrect because continental drift is the movement of the continents on Earth over time.

Question 37

Choice (A) is the correct answer. Crossing-over is a process that occurs in prophase I of meiosis when the homologous chromosomes of a pair align and parts of the paternal and maternal chromosomes are exchanged. This process leads to genetic combinations in the gametes that are different from the genetic makeup of either parent and thus increases genetic variation. None of the other options have anything to do with crossing over.

Question 38

Choice (A) is the correct answer. Of the biomes listed, the highest net primary productivity is found in estuaries. Net primary productivity is determined by calculating the total or gross primary productivity by the producers (generally plants) and subtracting the amount of respiration by those organisms.

Question 39

Choice (B) is the correct answer. During muscle contraction, myosin binds and hydrolyzes ATP, which provides energy for the movement of myosin relative to actin. Options A, C, D, and E have other roles in the cellular metabolism.

Question 40

Choice (D) is the correct answer. Of all of the organelles listed, only mitochondria and chloroplasts are capable of ATP production.

Question 41

Choice (E) is the correct answer. Antidiuretic hormone (ADH), also known as vasopressin, functions to retain water in the body and to constrict blood vessels. When a person is dehydrated, ADH is released and the effect on the kidneys is to increase water reabsorption and concentrate the urine. Option A is incorrect because the water reabsorption in the loop of Henle is driven by the osmolarity gradient between the nephron and the surrounding tissue. Option B is incorrect because permeability of the collecting duct to water increases in response to ADH. Option C is incorrect because, by increasing water reabsorption, the blood volume will be maintained or will increase. Option D is incorrect because it is the opposite of what will occur.

Question 42

Choice (A) is the correct answer. Increasing the number of stomata on the upper surface of a leaf will result in more evaporation from the leaf surface as the stomata open to allow CO_2 into the leaf spaces. Option B is incorrect because the number of stomata on the upper surface of the leaf will not affect the stomata on the undersurface of the leaf. Option C is incorrect because the rate of respiration will not be affected by having more stomata on the upper surface of the leaf. Option D is incorrect because transpiration will increase, not decrease, since there will be more evaporation of water from the leaf. Option E is incorrect because the number of stomata does not affect the dropping of leaves by deciduous trees in the autumn.

Question 43

Choice (A) is the correct answer. The average energy transfer from one trophic level to the next higher trophic level is only about 10 percent. The rest of the energy is generally lost as metabolic heat. Option B is incorrect because an organism can occupy more than one tropic level—an example is a bear that eats berries (primary consumer) and also fish (secondary consumer). Option C is incorrect because consumers do not store more energy than producers; the trophic levels for consumers store less energy than is stored by the trophic level that contains producers. Option D is incorrect because detritivores do not provide energy; they release nutrients back into the environment. Option E is incorrect because tertiary-level consumers are not more numerous than producers.

Question 44

Choice (A) is the correct answer. We are told that hunters began killing the predators in 1910. Before 1910 the population was relatively stable, and since the predators were present then, it is reasonable to assume that the predators had a role in the maintenance of the deer population at the carrying capacity. With the reduction in predators after 1920, the deer population increased until it could no longer be sustained (1925 drop), and there is no stability in the population size between 1925 and 1940.

Question 45

Choice (B) is the correct answer. Note that this question has a negative stem. Resumption of hunting predators (B) would eliminate or reduce the risk of predation and should result in an increased deer population. Overgrazing of the land by the deer (A) could lead to a significant decrease in the population, since food would become limiting.

Fires (C) could contribute to the decrease because they could also eliminate food. A disease epidemic (D) could have a significant impact on the population size. A new competitor introduced into the ecosystem (E) could also have a significant impact on the population size.

Question 46

Choice (D) is the correct answer. Of the statements given, the one that is supported by the data is option D. Prior to 1910 predators presumably kept the deer population below the maximum carrying capacity of the environment, and when those predators were removed the deer population size presumably increased above the maximum carrying capacity. None of the others can be supported by the data.

Question 47

Choice (E) is the correct answer. After 1 hour the gas filling the balloon is most likely carbon dioxide produced by yeast that are undergoing fermentation. Options A, B, C, and D are not the products of metabolism by yeast.

Question 48

Choice (A) is the correct answer. Molasses is the source of the sugar for the yeast. Of the options given, only sucrose is a sugar. The other macromolecules (B, C, D, and E) can serve as energy sources when sugar is not available, but sugar is the most easily metabolized and is present in the molasses syrup in greater amounts.

Question 49

Choice (B) is the correct answer. The experiment was conducted with warm water. We are not given the specific temperature; however, it would be reasonable to assume that the temperature is higher than room temperature (70°F or 21°C). If the flask cooled, it is likely that cellular metabolism would proceed more slowly, and thus the gas would form more slowly.

Question 50

Choice (E) is the correct answer. The process producing the gas is fermentation. Fermentation is a particular type of cellular respiration that produces energy from the breakdown of sugar and releases carbon dioxide.

Question 51

Choice (A) is the correct answer. If the yeast had been boiled prior to the experiment, all of the enzymes in the yeast cells would be denatured and the yeast cells would have been killed. They would be unable to undergo fermentation or any other metabolic function. The sugars would remain and no gas would form.

Question 52

Choice (D) is the correct answer. The human DNA polymerase activity is represented by the dashed line. The line indicates that the maximum reaction rate is just below 40°C, making 37°C the best answer. Since this is close to body temperature, it is not surprising that the optimal range of a human enzyme would be at this temperature.

Question 53

Choice (A) is the correct answer. The line for the algal DNA polymerase activity is the line with activity at the lowest temperatures. It shows the reaction rate increasing from approximately 15°C to approximately 36°C and then declining. Of the options given, the most reasonable explanation is that temperature affected the reaction rate. Options B, C, D, and E are incorrect because while they are true statements, they do not explain the change in activity.

Question 54

Choice (B) is the correct answer. Each of the enzymes shows a decline in reaction rate at temperatures above the optimum, and at the highest temperatures they all show a point with no further activity. Enzymes are proteins and have a specific tertiary structure that is required for catalysis to occur. When the tertiary structure is disrupted, the enzyme is denatured. Enzymes can be denatured by high temperatures and other conditions, such as changes in pH. Option A is incorrect because enzymes may have different optimum temperatures, as the data suggest. Option C is incorrect because while it is a true statement, it does not explain the decline in activity. Option D is incorrect because low temperatures do not generally disrupt the tertiary structure. Option E is incorrect because the amino acids remain intact.

Question 55

Choice (E) is the correct answer. The data indicate that the algal enzyme is functional from 15°C to around 40°C. The human enzyme is functional from 30°C to around 44°C. The most reasonable explanation is that the human enzyme works best within the range of normal human body temperatures. Humans regulate their body temperature metabolically, and algae and bacteria do not. Option A is incorrect because photosynthesis does not affect this enzyme. Option B is incorrect because it does not address the data. Option C is incorrect because while it is a true statement, it does not address the data. Option D is incorrect because humans are endotherms that regulate body temperatures via metabolic and physiological mechanisms.

Question 56

Choice (D) is the correct answer. Based on the data, the most reasonable prediction is that the enzymes are not identical; in other words, their primary structure is different. The primary structure of a protein is the sequence of amino acids. Option A is incorrect because bacteria do not have mitochondrial genes. Option B is incorrect because the enzymes all catalyze DNA polymerization. Option C is incorrect because the base-pairing rules of DNA are the same in all organisms. Option E is incorrect because DNA polymerase functions in the nucleus of eukaryotes, which include humans and algae.

Question 57

Choice (A) is the correct answer. The values for 30°C show an increase in the first three hours and then a steady rate of 140, so the most reasonable graph is shown in option A.

Question 58

Choice (C) is the correct answer. If the reading were taken at 40°C at 7.5 hours, it would most likely be between 130 (7 hours) and 120 (8 hours). The only option that is between those two values is 125% (option C).

Question 59

Choice (C) is the correct answer. The control temperature is 25°C. In the summary of the experiment, it is stated that the rates are given as a percentage of the rate at 25°C, which is therefore 100 percent and is the rate to which the others are compared.

Question 60

Choice (E) is the correct answer. In the data table, there is no respiration in peas maintained for eight hours at a temperature of 50°C. The lack of respiration would indicate the pea seedlings have died.

Question 61

Choice (B) is the correct answer. The options given are trophic levels. The organisms whose growth is limited by light intensity and nitrate availability are photosynthetic—mainly plants. Plants are producers.

Question 62

Choice (C) is the correct answer. Rabbits that eat lettuce are acting as primary consumers (sometimes called herbivores). Primary consumers feed directly on producers (lettuce).

Question 63

Choice (D) is the correct answer. Fish that eat herbivorous snails are secondary consumers. The snails are primary consumers (note that they are herbivorous snails), and the fish eating those snails are thus secondary consumers.

Question 64

Choice (D) is the correct answer. Organisms that maintain a constant body temperature metabolically are endotherms. Mammals and birds are generally considered to be endotherms. Of the animals listed, the only endotherm is option D, the ostrich. The animals in options A, B, C, and E may adjust their body temperatures somewhat through their behaviors but not through their metabolism.

Question 65

Choice (A) is the correct answer. In a food chain, only approximately 10 percent of the energy is transferred from one trophic level to the next. The trophic level with the greatest amount of available energy is that containing the producers. If people act as primary consumers, more of the available energy will be incorporated than if people act as members of the higher tropic levels. All meats, fish, and dairy products (B, C, D, and E) would fall into one of the consumer trophic levels, and the people consuming those products would belong to a higher trophic level.

Question 66

Choice (A) is the correct answer. A population includes organisms of the same species in a particular location. The Douglas fir trees along a river bank constitute a population. Option B is incorrect because it consists of all the populations of a particular toad species found on the continent of North America. Option C is incorrect because the various individuals of a subspecies of garter snake belong to more than one population. It is possible that a particular subspecies would exist as a single population, but that would only occur in rare instances. Option D is incorrect because it includes more than one species. Option E is incorrect because it includes more than one species as well.

Question 67

Choice (B) is the correct answer. Note that this question has a negative stem. The kingdom Plantae includes multicellular, eukaryotic organisms that have a large central vacuole, are generally photosynthetic, and have cell walls composed of cellulose. Of the organisms listed, the only one that does <u>not</u> meet those criteria is B, fungi. The fungi are classified into a separate kingdom, the kingdom Fungi.

Question 68

Choice (B) is the correct answer. The question states that there are some strains of mosquitoes that are not susceptible to DDT and asks for the most reasonable explanation. Of the options given, B is the most reasonable explanation: that mosquitoes that were resistant to DDT were able to survive and reproduce, thereby passing on the resistance to their offspring. This is an example of selection for a trait. Option A is incorrect because DDT is not an antigen; it attacks the neurons of the insects. Option C is incorrect because whether DDT degrades is not relevant to resistance to new applications of the chemical. Moreover, is a very long-lasting chemical, which is why it was banned for use in the United States. Option D is incorrect because DDT does not interfere with the synthesis of RNA. Option E is incorrect because DDT does not have a positive impact on larval development.

Question 69

Choice (D) is the correct answer. The diagram of the mountain range shows the wind blowing from west to east. The question asks why there is different vegetation on the western slope of the mountain than on the eastern slope. In the west, the wind brings moist air to the western slope, where it rises and cools. The moisture condenses and drops as precipitation on the western slope. The vegetation will be denser on that slope due to increased precipitation (or moisture) and will likely be composed of different species than on the drier eastern slope. The amount of sunlight will be similar on both slopes of the mountain.

Question 70

Choice (E) is the correct answer. If a species shows little evolutionary change over time, the most reasonable explanation is that it exists in a stable environment. The stable environment would not be adding any new selective pressure to the population. Option A is incorrect because inbreeding would not purge harmful genes and would not maintain a population over a long period of time with little change. Option B is incorrect because genetic variation helps to maintain species over time. There are no species with a zero mutation rate. Option C is incorrect because homozygosity is not necessary for maintaining genetic stability. Option D is incorrect because there is a common genetic code; the DNA of the species is not different from the DNA of other species.

Question 71

Choice (E) is the correct answer. Vitamins A, D, E, and K are all required by humans (making A incorrect) and cannot be synthesized by humans (making D incorrect). What these vitamins all have in common is that they are fat-soluble. Because these vitamins are stored in fat, humans do not need to consume them daily. Vitamins have varied functions but typically are required for particular chemical reactions. Vitamin A is important for vision (making B incorrect), among other functions. Vitamin D is involved in absorption of calcium and other minerals, but not all of the other vitamins are. Vitamin E is an antioxidant, among other functions and is not significant in bone synthesis (making C incorrect). Vitamin K is required for proteins involved in blood coagulation. Some vitamins are water-soluble, such as B-complex vitamins and vitamin C. These must be ingested daily.

Question 72

Choice (E) is the correct answer. Reptiles that thrive in desert environments must have mechanisms to deal with low moisture conditions and high temperatures. Some deserts are cooler, but they still are very dry. Keratinized skin helps to prevent desiccation, and using uric acid to excrete nitrogenous wastes conserves water. Option A is incorrect because glandular skin will not conserve water and hibernation is not typical of desert dwellers. Option B is incorrect because cartilaginous endoskeletons are not found in reptiles. Protective coloration is found in many organisms and is not peculiar to deserts. Option C is incorrect because reptiles do not have four-chambered hearts or endothermy. Option D is incorrect because advanced sensory systems will not confer a specific advantage to a desert reptile as opposed to a forest-dwelling reptile and reptiles typically have internal fertilization.

Question 73

Choice (C) is the correct answer. Note that this question has a negative stem. Energy flows through trophic levels in an ecosystem. The energy from sunlight is converted to chemical energy by producers (plants) (A), decomposers break down dead organic material making the matter and energy available for other organisms (B), approximately 90 percent of the energy in each trophic level is lost as heat as matter and energy move between trophic levels (D), and consumers eat producers or other consumers (E), which transfers matter an energy. The option that does not refer to energy flow is C.

Question 74

Choice (B) is the correct answer. The life cycle of a fern involves two stages: the gametophyte and the sporophyte. The gametophyte stage (D) produces the gametes (C) in either archegonia (E) (female gametes) or antheridia (male gametes). None of these have vascular tissues. After fertilization, the vascular sporophyte (B) grows out of the gametophyte. The sporophyte produces haploid spores (A), which then grow into new gametophytes.

Question 75

Choice (A) is the correct answer. The greater the amount of photosynthesis, the more CO_2 is removed from the atmosphere. Photosynthesis requires sunlight and liquid water. Plants living in environments with less solar radiation will have a lower photosynthetic output than plants living in environments with strong solar radiation. Of the options, the tundra, particularly the Arctic tundra, has low levels of solar radiation and no liquid water for several months of the year, and hence low rates of photosynthesis.

Question 76

Choice (A) is the correct answer. The lowest amount of primary productivity in the ocean will occur in the area that receives the least amount of solar radiation. The abyssal zone, at the bottom of the ocean, will receive the lowest level because the sunlight cannot penetrate to that depth.

Question 77

Choice (C) is the correct answer. Organisms that live in the abyssal zone receive almost no light, live under very high pressure, and live at low temperatures (about 4°C). Statements I and II are correct. Statement III, the requirement for high light intensity, is incorrect.

Question 78

Choice (E) is the correct answer. Based on the information provided, plant I is always attached to plant II by natural root grafts; that is, the roots of plant I are attached to plant II. The main function of the roots in plants is to absorb water and nutrients. Plants that undergo photosynthesis are normally green due to the chlorophyll that capture light in the chloroplasts. Albino plants cannot carry out photosynthesis to obtain energy, yet the albino plants are getting sufficient nutrients to flower and produce seeds. Altogether this suggests that plant I is getting some materials from plant II. Option A is incorrect because there is no evidence for a defective vascular system. Option B is incorrect because there is no evidence that plant I only takes up water through its roots. Option C is incorrect because there is no information about pollination. Option D is incorrect because plant I is living on plant II, so if the environment is suitable for plant II then it is suitable for plant I.

Question 79

Choice (A) is the correct answer. The information provided states that plant II specimens that do not have plant I attached are more vigorous, thus plant II should grow better in the absence of plant I. Option B is incorrect because plant II is found without plant I. Option C is incorrect because plant II does not require attachment to another plant for survival, and is harmed by the attachment of other plants. Option D is incorrect because plant II is more vigorous without plant I attached, so the relationship does not benefit plant II. Option E is incorrect because albinism is a genetic characteristic; it does not spread from plant to plant.

Question 80

Choice (C) is the correct answer. The fact that the albino plants flower and produce seeds means that they are getting sufficient nutrients, and the only reasonable conclusion is that plant I is getting this material from plant II. Option A is incorrect because, in the absence of chlorophyll, there is no photosynthesis in the leaves of plant I. Option B is incorrect because albinism is a genetic condition. Option D is incorrect because albinism is genetically controlled, regardless of whether plant I is a parasite. Option E is incorrect because albinism is not caused by transduction.

Question 81

Choice (A) is the correct answer. The hydrolysis of ATP (adenosine triphosphate) results in ADP (adenosine diphosphate) and the release of a phosphate group (A).

Question 82

Choice (E) is the correct answer. Glucose is the molecule that is metabolized by glycolysis and aerobic respiration to produce ATP.

Question 83

Choice (C) is the correct answer. The basic structural unit of proteins is an amino acid (C), identified by an amino group and a carboxyl group.

Question 84

Choice (B) is the correct answer. Nucleotides are composed of a nitrogenous base, a sugar, and a phosphate group.

Question 85

Choice (D) is the correct answer. An enzyme is a protein that lowers the energy of activation of a chemical reaction, allowing the reaction to proceed. A hormone (A) regulates homeostasis via feedback loops; a nucleotide (B) is a subunit of DNA and RNA; a cofactor (C) is a molecule that is often required by an enzyme, but cannot catalyze a reaction in the absence of the enzyme; and antibodies (E) are proteins that help protect the body from pathogens.

Question 86

Choice (C) is the correct answer. The initial reactant in glycolysis is glucose, which has the chemical formula $C_6H_{12}O_6$.

Question 87

Choice (A) is the correct answer. Note that this question has a negative stem. The nucleolus is a structure within the nucleus of a eukaryotic cell that is not bound by a membrane. The nuclear envelope (B) is the membrane surrounding the nucleus; the endoplasmic reticulum (C) is part of the endomembrane system and is continuous with the membrane of the nucleus; and mitochondria (D) and chloroplasts (E) are both organelles surrounded by membranes.

Question 88

Choice (C) is the correct answer. All lipids are hydrophobic, which means they do not dissolve in water. Lipids are generally not acidic (A) nor basic, they are typically not negatively charged (B) nor positively charged, they are not made from amino acids (D), and only some lipids are phosphorylated (E).

Question 89

Choice (E) is the correct answer. If a man shows the recessive condition for an autosomal trait, he has two recessive alleles for that trait. Even though only one of the alleles will be contained in sperm cell produced by the man, the correct answer is that all of the sperm cells, or 100 percent, produced will have a recessive allele.

Question 90

Choice (D) is the correct answer. A defining characteristic of prokaryotes is that they do not have membrane-bound organelles. All cells have a plasma membrane, cytoplasm, and genetic material (DNA), but only eukaryotes have membrane-bound organelles such as mitochondria or a nucleus within the cell. Option A is incorrect because prokaryotes also contain other structures, such as ribosomes and they do not have a nucleus. Option B is incorrect because prokaryotes do not contain mitochondria. Option C is incorrect because prokaryotes lack a true nucleus. Option E is incorrect because prokaryotes do contain DNA.

Question 91

Choice (D) is the correct answer. Restriction fragment length polymorphisms (RFLPs) are created by digesting DNA samples with known restriction enzymes to produce fragments of different lengths. The fragments are then separated by gel electrophoresis, and the resulting patterns can be compared across individuals. Of the options given, only D involves DNA. There are additional methods of DNA fingerprinting, but none of those are given as options.

Question 92

Choice (E) is the correct answer. The Golgi apparatus is an organelle that is part of the cell's endomembrane system. It functions to modify and package proteins for secretion from the cell. Option A is incorrect because the Golgi apparatus would be more extensive in a secretory cell than in a cell specialized for absorption. Option B is incorrect because the Golgi apparatus does not contain ribosomes; this describes the endoplasmic reticulum (ER). Option C is incorrect because the Golgi apparatus does not contain hydrolytic enzymes; this describes the lysosome. Option D is incorrect because the Golgi apparatus does not produce hydrogen peroxide; this describes the peroxisome.

Question 93

Choice (E) is the correct answer. Both mitochondria and chloroplasts can synthesize ATP. Option A is incorrect because light-capturing pigments are found in chloroplasts but not mitochondria. Option B is incorrect because mitochondria produce CO_2 but chloroplasts do not. Option C is incorrect because oxygen is produced in chloroplasts but not in mitochondria. Option D is incorrect because glucose is synthesized in chloroplasts but not in mitochondria.

Question 94

Choice (C) is the correct answer. A protein that will be secreted is produced by the ribosome on the rough endoplasmic reticulum (structure 4), then goes to the Golgi apparatus (structure 3), and then is packaged into a vesicle (structure 2) for secretion. Structure 1 is the plasma membrane; structure 5 is the chromatin in the nucleus; structure 6 is the smooth endoplasmic reticulum; and structure 7 is the mitochondrion. None of those structures are directly involved in protein secretion.

Question 95

Choice (E) is the correct answer. Phospholipids form the lipid bilayer of the cell or plasma membrane. Chromatin (A) is the name for the DNA during interphase when it is not condensed into chromosomes. Ribosomes (B) are the site of protein synthesis. The cytoskeleton (C) is an intracellular system composed of protein filaments. The spindle apparatus (D) forms during mitosis and is also composed of protein filaments.

Question 96

Choice (E) is the correct answer. The information given suggests that albinism is recessive because the ratio of normal to albino is 3:1. Since all of the albinos in this situation are male, it is reasonable to conclude that the mode of inheritance is sex-linked recessive rather than autosomal recessive.

Question 97

Choice (C) is the correct answer. Both anaerobic and aerobic cellular respiration produce ATP. Aerobic respiration produces more ATP than anaerobic respiration does. Option A is incorrect because the primary fuel source in both pathways is glucose. Option B is incorrect because glycolysis always takes place in the cytoplasm outside of the mitochondria. Option D is incorrect because anaerobic respiration occurs in both prokaryotes and eukaryotes, in addition to aerobic respiration. Option E is incorrect because photons are not required for cellular respiration.

Question 98

Choice (C) is the correct answer. The result of the infection with the retrovirus is increased cell division in the (cancer) cells that contain viral genes. Stimulation of cell division is thus the most likely function of protein X. Option A is incorrect because there is no evidence of an immune response. Option B is incorrect because the cell undergoes division, not death. Option D is incorrect because the virus has been incorporated into the host cell and is not released again. Option E is incorrect because increasing ATP production would not stimulate excess cell division that is characteristic of cancer.

Question 99

Choice (D) is the correct answer. Retroviruses have the enzyme reverse transcriptase, which uses RNA as a template and allows genetic information to flow from RNA to DNA in the opposite direction of its usual flow from DNA to RNA. Option A is incorrect because nucleic acids are not unique to retroviruses. Option B is incorrect because retroviruses do not typically infect prokaryotic cells, and infecting eukaryotic cells is not a unique characteristic. Option C is incorrect because all viruses possess protein coats. Option E is incorrect because rapid mutation is not unique to retroviruses.

Question 100

Choice (B) is the correct answer. Based on the diagram, infection with the retrovirus resulted in the random insertion of the viral genome near a potentially cancer-causing gene, which resulted in the production of cancer cells. Option A is incorrect because only one virus is shown, so no conclusion can be drawn about all viruses. Option C is incorrect because there is no information about pollutants given. Option D is incorrect because the diagram shows that infection with one virus is sufficient to result in cancer cells. Option E is incorrect because the viral RNA itself is not attached to DNA in the cancer cells or in the parent cell; it is the DNA copied from the viral RNA that is incorporated into the host DNA.

SAT Subject Tests™

1 **Your Name:**
(Print)

Last   First   M.I.

I agree to the conditions on the front and back of the SAT Subject Tests™ book. I also agree with the SAT Test Security and Fairness policies and understand that any violation of these policies will result in score cancellation and may result in reporting of certain violations to law enforcement.

Signature: _____   Today's Date: ___/___/___
                                                              MM DD YY

Home Address:
(Print)
Number and Street   City   State/Country   Zip Code
Phone: ( )   **Test Center:** _____
                        (Print)   City   State/Country

2 **YOUR NAME**

Last Name (First 6 Letters) | First Name (First 4 Letters) | Mid. Init.

3 **DATE OF BIRTH**

MONTH	DAY	YEAR
○ Jan		
○ Feb		
○ Mar		
○ Apr		
○ May		
○ Jun		
○ Jul		
○ Aug		
○ Sep		
○ Oct		
○ Nov		
○ Dec		

4 **REGISTRATION NUMBER**
(Copy from Admission Ticket.)

Important: Fill in items 8 and 9 exactly as shown on the back of test book.

7 **TEST BOOK SERIAL NUMBER**
(Copy from front of test book.)

8 **BOOK CODE**
(Copy and grid as on back of test book.)

5 **ZIP CODE**

6 **TEST CENTER**
(Supplied by Test Center Supervisor.)

9 **BOOK ID**
(Copy from back of test book.)

PLEASE MAKE SURE to fill in these fields completely and correctly. If they are not correct, we won't be able to score your test(s)!

FOR OFFICIAL USE ONLY

103648-77191 • NS1114C1085 • Printed in U.S.A.

© 2015 The College Board. College Board, SAT, and the acorn logo are registered trademarks of the College Board. SAT Subject Tests is a trademark owned by the College Board.

194415-001   1 2 3 4 5 A B C D E   Printed in the USA   ISD11312   783175

PLEASE DO NOT WRITE IN THIS AREA   **SERIAL #**

23459 College Board 15b-10820-Text

○ Literature ○ Mathematics Level 1 ○ German ○ Chinese Listening ○ Japanese Listening
○ Biology E ○ Mathematics Level 2 ○ Italian ○ French Listening ○ Korean Listening
○ Biology M ○ U.S. History ○ Latin ○ German Listening ○ Spanish Listening
○ Chemistry ○ World History ○ Modern Hebrew
○ Physics ○ French ○ Spanish

Background Questions: ① ② ③ ④ ⑤ ⑥ ⑦ ⑧ ⑨

1–100. (A) (B) (C) (D) (E) answer bubbles for questions 1 through 100.

PLEASE MAKE SURE to fill in these fields completely and correctly. If they are not correct, we won't be able to score your test(s)!

7 TEST BOOK SERIAL NUMBER (Copy from front of test book.)

8 BOOK CODE (Copy and grid as on back of test book.)

9 BOOK ID (Copy from back of test book.)

Quality Assurance Mark ●

Chemistry *Fill in circle CE only if II is correct explanation of I.

	I	II	CE*		I	II	CE*
101	(T) (F)	(T) (F)	○	109	(T) (F)	(T) (F)	○
102	(T) (F)	(T) (F)	○	110	(T) (F)	(T) (F)	○
103	(T) (F)	(T) (F)	○	111	(T) (F)	(T) (F)	○
104	(T) (F)	(T) (F)	○	112	(T) (F)	(T) (F)	○
105	(T) (F)	(T) (F)	○	113	(T) (F)	(T) (F)	○
106	(T) (F)	(T) (F)	○	114	(T) (F)	(T) (F)	○
107	(T) (F)	(T) (F)	○	115	(T) (F)	(T) (F)	○
108	(T) (F)	(T) (F)	○				

FOR OFFICIAL USE ONLY

R/C	W/S1	FS/S2	CS/S3	WS

CERTIFICATION STATEMENT
Copy the statement below and sign your name as you would an official document.

I hereby agree to the conditions set forth online at sat.collegeboard.org and in any paper registration materials given to me and certify that I am the person whose name, address and signature appear on this answer sheet.

Signature _____ Date _____

23459 College Board 15b-10820-Text

- ○ Literature
- ○ Biology E
- ○ Biology M
- ○ Chemistry
- ○ Physics
- ○ Mathematics Level 1
- ○ Mathematics Level 2
- ○ U.S. History
- ○ World History
- ○ French
- ○ German
- ○ Italian
- ○ Latin
- ○ Modern Hebrew
- ○ Spanish
- ○ Chinese Listening
- ○ French Listening
- ○ German Listening
- ○ Japanese Listening
- ○ Korean Listening
- ○ Spanish Listening

Background Questions: ① ② ③ ④ ⑤ ⑥ ⑦ ⑧ ⑨

PLEASE MAKE SURE to fill in these fields completely and correctly. If they are not correct, we won't be able to score your test(s)!

1–100. A B C D E answer grid

Quality Assurance Mark ●

7 TEST BOOK SERIAL NUMBER (Copy from front of test book.)

8 BOOK CODE (Copy and grid as on back of test book.)

9 BOOK ID (Copy from back of test book.)

Chemistry *Fill in circle CE only if II is correct explanation of I.

	I	II	CE*		I	II	CE*
101	T F	T F	○	109	T F	T F	○
102	T F	T F	○	110	T F	T F	○
103	T F	T F	○	111	T F	T F	○
104	T F	T F	○	112	T F	T F	○
105	T F	T F	○	113	T F	T F	○
106	T F	T F	○	114	T F	T F	○
107	T F	T F	○	115	T F	T F	○
108	T F	T F	○				

FOR OFFICIAL USE ONLY				
R/C	W/S1	FS/S2	CS/S3	WS

Page 3

○ Literature
○ Biology E
○ Biology M
○ Chemistry
○ Physics

○ Mathematics Level 1
○ Mathematics Level 2
○ U.S. History
○ World History
○ French

○ German
○ Italian
○ Latin
○ Modern Hebrew
○ Spanish

○ Chinese Listening
○ French Listening
○ German Listening

○ Japanese Listening
○ Korean Listening
○ Spanish Listening

Background Questions: ① ② ③ ④ ⑤ ⑥ ⑦ ⑧ ⑨

PLEASE MAKE SURE to fill in these fields completely and correctly. If they are not correct, we won't be able to score your test(s)!

Questions 1–100, options A B C D E each.

7 TEST BOOK SERIAL NUMBER
(Copy from front of test book.)
0 0 0 0 0 0
1 1 1 1 1 1
2 2 2 2 2 2
3 3 3 3 3 3
4 4 4 4 4 4
5 5 5 5 5 5
6 6 6 6 6 6
7 7 7 7 7 7
8 8 8 8 8 8
9 9 9 9 9 9

8 BOOK CODE
(Copy and grid as on back of test book.)
0 A 0
1 B 1
2 C 2
3 D 3
4 E 4
5 F 5
6 G 6
7 H 7
8 I 8
9 J 9
K
L
M
N
O
P
Q
R
S
T
U
V
W
X
Y
Z

9 BOOK ID
(Copy from back of test book.)

Quality Assurance Mark ●

Chemistry *Fill in circle CE only if II is correct explanation of I.

	I	II	CE*		I	II	CE*
101	T F	T F	○	109	T F	T F	○
102	T F	T F	○	110	T F	T F	○
103	T F	T F	○	111	T F	T F	○
104	T F	T F	○	112	T F	T F	○
105	T F	T F	○	113	T F	T F	○
106	T F	T F	○	114	T F	T F	○
107	T F	T F	○	115	T F	T F	○
108	T F	T F	○				

FOR OFFICIAL USE ONLY

R/C	W/S1	FS/S2	CS/S3	WS

Page 4

23459 College Board 15b-10820-Text

 **CollegeBoard**

SAT Subject Tests™

COMPLETE MARK ● **EXAMPLES OF INCOMPLETE MARKS**

You must use a No. 2 pencil and marks must be complete. Do not use a mechanical pencil. It is very important that you fill in the entire circle darkly and completely. If you change your response, erase as completely as possible. Incomplete marks or erasures may affect your score.

1 **Your Name:**
(Print)

Last   First   M.I.

I agree to the conditions on the front and back of the SAT Subject Tests™ book. I also agree with the SAT Test Security and Fairness policies and understand that any violation of these policies will result in score cancellation and may result in reporting of certain violations to law enforcement.

Signature: _____   Today's Date: __/__/__
                                                                              MM DD YY
Home Address: _____
(Print)   Number and Street   City   State/Country   Zip Code
Phone: ( )_____ **Test Center:** _____
                                    (Print)   City   State/Country

2 **YOUR NAME**

Last Name (First 6 Letters)   First Name (First 4 Letters)   Mid. Init.

3 **DATE OF BIRTH**

MONTH   DAY   YEAR

○ Jan
○ Feb
○ Mar
○ Apr
○ May
○ Jun
○ Jul
○ Aug
○ Sep
○ Oct
○ Nov
○ Dec

4 **REGISTRATION NUMBER**
(Copy from Admission Ticket.)

Important: Fill in items 8 and 9 exactly as shown on the back of test book.

7 **TEST BOOK SERIAL NUMBER**
(Copy from front of test book.)

8 **BOOK CODE**
(Copy and grid as on back of test book.)

9 **BOOK ID**
(Copy from back of test book.)

PLEASE MAKE SURE to fill in these fields completely and correctly. If they are not correct, we won't be able to score your test(s)!

5 **ZIP CODE**

6 **TEST CENTER**
(Supplied by Test Center Supervisor.)

FOR OFFICIAL USE ONLY

103648-77191 • NS1114C1085 • Printed in U.S.A.

© 2015 The College Board. College Board, SAT, and the acorn logo are registered trademarks of the College Board. SAT Subject Tests is a trademark owned by the College Board.

194415-001   1 2 3 4 5 A B C D E   Printed in the USA   ISD11312

783175

PLEASE DO NOT WRITE IN THIS AREA   **SERIAL #**

23459 College Board 15b-10820-Text

COMPLETE MARK ●	EXAMPLES OF INCOMPLETE MARKS Ⓐ ⓧ ⊖ ⓟ ◍ ⊘ ◎	You must use a No. 2 pencil and marks must be complete. Do not use a mechanical pencil. *It is very important that you fill in the entire circle darkly and completely. If you change your response, erase as completely as possible. Incomplete marks or erasures may affect your score.*

- ○ Literature
- ○ Biology E
- ○ Biology M
- ○ Chemistry
- ○ Physics

- ○ Mathematics Level 1
- ○ Mathematics Level 2
- ○ U.S. History
- ○ World History
- ○ French

- ○ German
- ○ Italian
- ○ Latin
- ○ Modern Hebrew
- ○ Spanish

- ○ Chinese Listening
- ○ French Listening
- ○ German Listening

- ○ Japanese Listening
- ○ Korean Listening
- ○ Spanish Listening

Background Questions: ① ② ③ ④ ⑤ ⑥ ⑦ ⑧ ⑨

Answer grid: questions 1–100, each with options A B C D E

PLEASE MAKE SURE to fill in these fields completely and correctly. If they are not correct, we won't be able to score your test(s)!

7 TEST BOOK SERIAL NUMBER (Copy from front of test book.)
0 0 0 0 0 0
1 1 1 1 1 1
2 2 2 2 2 2
3 3 3 3 3 3
4 4 4 4 4 4
5 5 5 5 5 5
6 6 6 6 6 6
7 7 7 7 7 7
8 8 8 8 8 8
9 9 9 9 9 9

8 BOOK CODE (Copy and grid as on back of test book.)
0 A 0
1 B 1
2 C 2
3 D 3
4 E 4
5 F 5
6 G 6
7 H 7
8 I 8
9 J 9
K
L
M
N
O
P
Q
R
S
T
U
V
W
X
Y
Z

9 BOOK ID (Copy from back of test book.)

Quality Assurance Mark ●

Chemistry *Fill in circle CE only if II is correct explanation of I.

	I	II	CE*		I	II	CE*
101	T F	T F	○	109	T F	T F	○
102	T F	T F	○	110	T F	T F	○
103	T F	T F	○	111	T F	T F	○
104	T F	T F	○	112	T F	T F	○
105	T F	T F	○	113	T F	T F	○
106	T F	T F	○	114	T F	T F	○
107	T F	T F	○	115	T F	T F	○
108	T F	T F	○				

FOR OFFICIAL USE ONLY				
R/C	W/S1	FS/S2	CS/S3	WS

CERTIFICATION STATEMENT
Copy the statement below and sign your name as you would an official document.

I hereby agree to the conditions set forth online at sat.collegeboard.org and in any paper registration materials given to me and certify that I am the person whose name, address and signature appear on this answer sheet.

Signature _____

Date _____

23459 College Board 15b-10820-Text

○ Literature
○ Biology E
○ Biology M
○ Chemistry
○ Physics

○ Mathematics Level 1
○ Mathematics Level 2
○ U.S. History
○ World History
○ French

○ German
○ Italian
○ Latin
○ Modern Hebrew
○ Spanish

○ Chinese Listening
○ French Listening
○ German Listening

○ Japanese Listening
○ Korean Listening
○ Spanish Listening

Background Questions: ① ② ③ ④ ⑤ ⑥ ⑦ ⑧ ⑨

PLEASE MAKE SURE to fill in these fields completely and correctly. If they are not correct, we won't be able to score your test(s)!

1 Ⓐ Ⓑ Ⓒ Ⓓ Ⓔ   26 Ⓐ Ⓑ Ⓒ Ⓓ Ⓔ   51 Ⓐ Ⓑ Ⓒ Ⓓ Ⓔ   76 Ⓐ Ⓑ Ⓒ Ⓓ Ⓔ
2 Ⓐ Ⓑ Ⓒ Ⓓ Ⓔ   27 Ⓐ Ⓑ Ⓒ Ⓓ Ⓔ   52 Ⓐ Ⓑ Ⓒ Ⓓ Ⓔ   77 Ⓐ Ⓑ Ⓒ Ⓓ Ⓔ
3 Ⓐ Ⓑ Ⓒ Ⓓ Ⓔ   28 Ⓐ Ⓑ Ⓒ Ⓓ Ⓔ   53 Ⓐ Ⓑ Ⓒ Ⓓ Ⓔ   78 Ⓐ Ⓑ Ⓒ Ⓓ Ⓔ
4 Ⓐ Ⓑ Ⓒ Ⓓ Ⓔ   29 Ⓐ Ⓑ Ⓒ Ⓓ Ⓔ   54 Ⓐ Ⓑ Ⓒ Ⓓ Ⓔ   79 Ⓐ Ⓑ Ⓒ Ⓓ Ⓔ
5 Ⓐ Ⓑ Ⓒ Ⓓ Ⓔ   30 Ⓐ Ⓑ Ⓒ Ⓓ Ⓔ   55 Ⓐ Ⓑ Ⓒ Ⓓ Ⓔ   80 Ⓐ Ⓑ Ⓒ Ⓓ Ⓔ
6 Ⓐ Ⓑ Ⓒ Ⓓ Ⓔ   31 Ⓐ Ⓑ Ⓒ Ⓓ Ⓔ   56 Ⓐ Ⓑ Ⓒ Ⓓ Ⓔ   81 Ⓐ Ⓑ Ⓒ Ⓓ Ⓔ
7 Ⓐ Ⓑ Ⓒ Ⓓ Ⓔ   32 Ⓐ Ⓑ Ⓒ Ⓓ Ⓔ   57 Ⓐ Ⓑ Ⓒ Ⓓ Ⓔ   82 Ⓐ Ⓑ Ⓒ Ⓓ Ⓔ
8 Ⓐ Ⓑ Ⓒ Ⓓ Ⓔ   33 Ⓐ Ⓑ Ⓒ Ⓓ Ⓔ   58 Ⓐ Ⓑ Ⓒ Ⓓ Ⓔ   83 Ⓐ Ⓑ Ⓒ Ⓓ Ⓔ
9 Ⓐ Ⓑ Ⓒ Ⓓ Ⓔ   34 Ⓐ Ⓑ Ⓒ Ⓓ Ⓔ   59 Ⓐ Ⓑ Ⓒ Ⓓ Ⓔ   84 Ⓐ Ⓑ Ⓒ Ⓓ Ⓔ
10 Ⓐ Ⓑ Ⓒ Ⓓ Ⓔ   35 Ⓐ Ⓑ Ⓒ Ⓓ Ⓔ   60 Ⓐ Ⓑ Ⓒ Ⓓ Ⓔ   85 Ⓐ Ⓑ Ⓒ Ⓓ Ⓔ
11 Ⓐ Ⓑ Ⓒ Ⓓ Ⓔ   36 Ⓐ Ⓑ Ⓒ Ⓓ Ⓔ   61 Ⓐ Ⓑ Ⓒ Ⓓ Ⓔ   86 Ⓐ Ⓑ Ⓒ Ⓓ Ⓔ
12 Ⓐ Ⓑ Ⓒ Ⓓ Ⓔ   37 Ⓐ Ⓑ Ⓒ Ⓓ Ⓔ   62 Ⓐ Ⓑ Ⓒ Ⓓ Ⓔ   87 Ⓐ Ⓑ Ⓒ Ⓓ Ⓔ
13 Ⓐ Ⓑ Ⓒ Ⓓ Ⓔ   38 Ⓐ Ⓑ Ⓒ Ⓓ Ⓔ   63 Ⓐ Ⓑ Ⓒ Ⓓ Ⓔ   88 Ⓐ Ⓑ Ⓒ Ⓓ Ⓔ
14 Ⓐ Ⓑ Ⓒ Ⓓ Ⓔ   39 Ⓐ Ⓑ Ⓒ Ⓓ Ⓔ   64 Ⓐ Ⓑ Ⓒ Ⓓ Ⓔ   89 Ⓐ Ⓑ Ⓒ Ⓓ Ⓔ
15 Ⓐ Ⓑ Ⓒ Ⓓ Ⓔ   40 Ⓐ Ⓑ Ⓒ Ⓓ Ⓔ   65 Ⓐ Ⓑ Ⓒ Ⓓ Ⓔ   90 Ⓐ Ⓑ Ⓒ Ⓓ Ⓔ
16 Ⓐ Ⓑ Ⓒ Ⓓ Ⓔ   41 Ⓐ Ⓑ Ⓒ Ⓓ Ⓔ   66 Ⓐ Ⓑ Ⓒ Ⓓ Ⓔ   91 Ⓐ Ⓑ Ⓒ Ⓓ Ⓔ
17 Ⓐ Ⓑ Ⓒ Ⓓ Ⓔ   42 Ⓐ Ⓑ Ⓒ Ⓓ Ⓔ   67 Ⓐ Ⓑ Ⓒ Ⓓ Ⓔ   92 Ⓐ Ⓑ Ⓒ Ⓓ Ⓔ
18 Ⓐ Ⓑ Ⓒ Ⓓ Ⓔ   43 Ⓐ Ⓑ Ⓒ Ⓓ Ⓔ   68 Ⓐ Ⓑ Ⓒ Ⓓ Ⓔ   93 Ⓐ Ⓑ Ⓒ Ⓓ Ⓔ
19 Ⓐ Ⓑ Ⓒ Ⓓ Ⓔ   44 Ⓐ Ⓑ Ⓒ Ⓓ Ⓔ   69 Ⓐ Ⓑ Ⓒ Ⓓ Ⓔ   94 Ⓐ Ⓑ Ⓒ Ⓓ Ⓔ
20 Ⓐ Ⓑ Ⓒ Ⓓ Ⓔ   45 Ⓐ Ⓑ Ⓒ Ⓓ Ⓔ   70 Ⓐ Ⓑ Ⓒ Ⓓ Ⓔ   95 Ⓐ Ⓑ Ⓒ Ⓓ Ⓔ
21 Ⓐ Ⓑ Ⓒ Ⓓ Ⓔ   46 Ⓐ Ⓑ Ⓒ Ⓓ Ⓔ   71 Ⓐ Ⓑ Ⓒ Ⓓ Ⓔ   96 Ⓐ Ⓑ Ⓒ Ⓓ Ⓔ
22 Ⓐ Ⓑ Ⓒ Ⓓ Ⓔ   47 Ⓐ Ⓑ Ⓒ Ⓓ Ⓔ   72 Ⓐ Ⓑ Ⓒ Ⓓ Ⓔ   97 Ⓐ Ⓑ Ⓒ Ⓓ Ⓔ
23 Ⓐ Ⓑ Ⓒ Ⓓ Ⓔ   48 Ⓐ Ⓑ Ⓒ Ⓓ Ⓔ   73 Ⓐ Ⓑ Ⓒ Ⓓ Ⓔ   98 Ⓐ Ⓑ Ⓒ Ⓓ Ⓔ
24 Ⓐ Ⓑ Ⓒ Ⓓ Ⓔ   49 Ⓐ Ⓑ Ⓒ Ⓓ Ⓔ   74 Ⓐ Ⓑ Ⓒ Ⓓ Ⓔ   99 Ⓐ Ⓑ Ⓒ Ⓓ Ⓔ
25 Ⓐ Ⓑ Ⓒ Ⓓ Ⓔ   50 Ⓐ Ⓑ Ⓒ Ⓓ Ⓔ   75 Ⓐ Ⓑ Ⓒ Ⓓ Ⓔ   100 Ⓐ Ⓑ Ⓒ Ⓓ Ⓔ

Quality Assurance Mark ●

8 BOOK CODE (Copy and grid as on back of test book.)

0	A	0
1	B	1
2	C	2
3	D	3
4	E	4
5	F	5
6	G	6
7	H	7
8	I	8
9	J	9
	K	
	L	
	M	
	N	
	O	
	P	
	Q	
	R	
	S	
	T	
	U	
	V	
	W	
	X	
	Y	
	Z	

7 TEST BOOK SERIAL NUMBER (Copy from front of test book.)

0 0 0 0 0 0
1 1 1 1 1 1
2 2 2 2 2 2
3 3 3 3 3 3
4 4 4 4 4 4
5 5 5 5 5 5
6 6 6 6 6 6
7 7 7 7 7 7
8 8 8 8 8 8
9 9 9 9 9 9

9 BOOK ID (Copy from back of test book.)

Chemistry *Fill in circle CE only if II is correct explanation of I.

	I	II	CE*		I	II	CE*
101	T F	T F	○	109	T F	T F	○
102	T F	T F	○	110	T F	T F	○
103	T F	T F	○	111	T F	T F	○
104	T F	T F	○	112	T F	T F	○
105	T F	T F	○	113	T F	T F	○
106	T F	T F	○	114	T F	T F	○
107	T F	T F	○	115	T F	T F	○
108	T F	T F	○				

FOR OFFICIAL USE ONLY				
R/C	W/S1	FS/S2	CS/S3	WS

Page 3

○ Literature
○ Biology E
○ Biology M
○ Chemistry
○ Physics

○ Mathematics Level 1
○ Mathematics Level 2
○ U.S. History
○ World History
○ French

○ German
○ Italian
○ Latin
○ Modern Hebrew
○ Spanish

○ Chinese Listening
○ French Listening
○ German Listening

○ Japanese Listening
○ Korean Listening
○ Spanish Listening

Background Questions: ① ② ③ ④ ⑤ ⑥ ⑦ ⑧ ⑨

PLEASE MAKE SURE to fill in these fields completely and correctly. If they are not correct, we won't be able to score your test(s)!

1 Ⓐ Ⓑ Ⓒ Ⓓ Ⓔ   26 Ⓐ Ⓑ Ⓒ Ⓓ Ⓔ   51 Ⓐ Ⓑ Ⓒ Ⓓ Ⓔ   76 Ⓐ Ⓑ Ⓒ Ⓓ Ⓔ
2 Ⓐ Ⓑ Ⓒ Ⓓ Ⓔ   27 Ⓐ Ⓑ Ⓒ Ⓓ Ⓔ   52 Ⓐ Ⓑ Ⓒ Ⓓ Ⓔ   77 Ⓐ Ⓑ Ⓒ Ⓓ Ⓔ
3 Ⓐ Ⓑ Ⓒ Ⓓ Ⓔ   28 Ⓐ Ⓑ Ⓒ Ⓓ Ⓔ   53 Ⓐ Ⓑ Ⓒ Ⓓ Ⓔ   78 Ⓐ Ⓑ Ⓒ Ⓓ Ⓔ
4 Ⓐ Ⓑ Ⓒ Ⓓ Ⓔ   29 Ⓐ Ⓑ Ⓒ Ⓓ Ⓔ   54 Ⓐ Ⓑ Ⓒ Ⓓ Ⓔ   79 Ⓐ Ⓑ Ⓒ Ⓓ Ⓔ
5 Ⓐ Ⓑ Ⓒ Ⓓ Ⓔ   30 Ⓐ Ⓑ Ⓒ Ⓓ Ⓔ   55 Ⓐ Ⓑ Ⓒ Ⓓ Ⓔ   80 Ⓐ Ⓑ Ⓒ Ⓓ Ⓔ
6 Ⓐ Ⓑ Ⓒ Ⓓ Ⓔ   31 Ⓐ Ⓑ Ⓒ Ⓓ Ⓔ   56 Ⓐ Ⓑ Ⓒ Ⓓ Ⓔ   81 Ⓐ Ⓑ Ⓒ Ⓓ Ⓔ
7 Ⓐ Ⓑ Ⓒ Ⓓ Ⓔ   32 Ⓐ Ⓑ Ⓒ Ⓓ Ⓔ   57 Ⓐ Ⓑ Ⓒ Ⓓ Ⓔ   82 Ⓐ Ⓑ Ⓒ Ⓓ Ⓔ
8 Ⓐ Ⓑ Ⓒ Ⓓ Ⓔ   33 Ⓐ Ⓑ Ⓒ Ⓓ Ⓔ   58 Ⓐ Ⓑ Ⓒ Ⓓ Ⓔ   83 Ⓐ Ⓑ Ⓒ Ⓓ Ⓔ
9 Ⓐ Ⓑ Ⓒ Ⓓ Ⓔ   34 Ⓐ Ⓑ Ⓒ Ⓓ Ⓔ   59 Ⓐ Ⓑ Ⓒ Ⓓ Ⓔ   84 Ⓐ Ⓑ Ⓒ Ⓓ Ⓔ
10 Ⓐ Ⓑ Ⓒ Ⓓ Ⓔ   35 Ⓐ Ⓑ Ⓒ Ⓓ Ⓔ   60 Ⓐ Ⓑ Ⓒ Ⓓ Ⓔ   85 Ⓐ Ⓑ Ⓒ Ⓓ Ⓔ
11 Ⓐ Ⓑ Ⓒ Ⓓ Ⓔ   36 Ⓐ Ⓑ Ⓒ Ⓓ Ⓔ   61 Ⓐ Ⓑ Ⓒ Ⓓ Ⓔ   86 Ⓐ Ⓑ Ⓒ Ⓓ Ⓔ
12 Ⓐ Ⓑ Ⓒ Ⓓ Ⓔ   37 Ⓐ Ⓑ Ⓒ Ⓓ Ⓔ   62 Ⓐ Ⓑ Ⓒ Ⓓ Ⓔ   87 Ⓐ Ⓑ Ⓒ Ⓓ Ⓔ
13 Ⓐ Ⓑ Ⓒ Ⓓ Ⓔ   38 Ⓐ Ⓑ Ⓒ Ⓓ Ⓔ   63 Ⓐ Ⓑ Ⓒ Ⓓ Ⓔ   88 Ⓐ Ⓑ Ⓒ Ⓓ Ⓔ
14 Ⓐ Ⓑ Ⓒ Ⓓ Ⓔ   39 Ⓐ Ⓑ Ⓒ Ⓓ Ⓔ   64 Ⓐ Ⓑ Ⓒ Ⓓ Ⓔ   89 Ⓐ Ⓑ Ⓒ Ⓓ Ⓔ
15 Ⓐ Ⓑ Ⓒ Ⓓ Ⓔ   40 Ⓐ Ⓑ Ⓒ Ⓓ Ⓔ   65 Ⓐ Ⓑ Ⓒ Ⓓ Ⓔ   90 Ⓐ Ⓑ Ⓒ Ⓓ Ⓔ
16 Ⓐ Ⓑ Ⓒ Ⓓ Ⓔ   41 Ⓐ Ⓑ Ⓒ Ⓓ Ⓔ   66 Ⓐ Ⓑ Ⓒ Ⓓ Ⓔ   91 Ⓐ Ⓑ Ⓒ Ⓓ Ⓔ
17 Ⓐ Ⓑ Ⓒ Ⓓ Ⓔ   42 Ⓐ Ⓑ Ⓒ Ⓓ Ⓔ   67 Ⓐ Ⓑ Ⓒ Ⓓ Ⓔ   92 Ⓐ Ⓑ Ⓒ Ⓓ Ⓔ
18 Ⓐ Ⓑ Ⓒ Ⓓ Ⓔ   43 Ⓐ Ⓑ Ⓒ Ⓓ Ⓔ   68 Ⓐ Ⓑ Ⓒ Ⓓ Ⓔ   93 Ⓐ Ⓑ Ⓒ Ⓓ Ⓔ
19 Ⓐ Ⓑ Ⓒ Ⓓ Ⓔ   44 Ⓐ Ⓑ Ⓒ Ⓓ Ⓔ   69 Ⓐ Ⓑ Ⓒ Ⓓ Ⓔ   94 Ⓐ Ⓑ Ⓒ Ⓓ Ⓔ
20 Ⓐ Ⓑ Ⓒ Ⓓ Ⓔ   45 Ⓐ Ⓑ Ⓒ Ⓓ Ⓔ   70 Ⓐ Ⓑ Ⓒ Ⓓ Ⓔ   95 Ⓐ Ⓑ Ⓒ Ⓓ Ⓔ
21 Ⓐ Ⓑ Ⓒ Ⓓ Ⓔ   46 Ⓐ Ⓑ Ⓒ Ⓓ Ⓔ   71 Ⓐ Ⓑ Ⓒ Ⓓ Ⓔ   96 Ⓐ Ⓑ Ⓒ Ⓓ Ⓔ
22 Ⓐ Ⓑ Ⓒ Ⓓ Ⓔ   47 Ⓐ Ⓑ Ⓒ Ⓓ Ⓔ   72 Ⓐ Ⓑ Ⓒ Ⓓ Ⓔ   97 Ⓐ Ⓑ Ⓒ Ⓓ Ⓔ
23 Ⓐ Ⓑ Ⓒ Ⓓ Ⓔ   48 Ⓐ Ⓑ Ⓒ Ⓓ Ⓔ   73 Ⓐ Ⓑ Ⓒ Ⓓ Ⓔ   98 Ⓐ Ⓑ Ⓒ Ⓓ Ⓔ
24 Ⓐ Ⓑ Ⓒ Ⓓ Ⓔ   49 Ⓐ Ⓑ Ⓒ Ⓓ Ⓔ   74 Ⓐ Ⓑ Ⓒ Ⓓ Ⓔ   99 Ⓐ Ⓑ Ⓒ Ⓓ Ⓔ
25 Ⓐ Ⓑ Ⓒ Ⓓ Ⓔ   50 Ⓐ Ⓑ Ⓒ Ⓓ Ⓔ   75 Ⓐ Ⓑ Ⓒ Ⓓ Ⓔ   100 Ⓐ Ⓑ Ⓒ Ⓓ Ⓔ

8 BOOK CODE
(Copy and grid as on back of test book.)

0	Ⓐ	0
1	Ⓑ	1
2	Ⓒ	2
3	Ⓓ	3
4	Ⓔ	4
5	Ⓕ	5
6	Ⓖ	6
7	Ⓗ	7
8	Ⓘ	8
9	Ⓙ	9
	Ⓚ	
	Ⓛ	
	Ⓜ	
	Ⓝ	
	Ⓞ	
	Ⓟ	
	Ⓠ	
	Ⓡ	
	Ⓢ	
	Ⓣ	
	Ⓤ	
	Ⓥ	
	Ⓦ	
	Ⓧ	
	Ⓨ	
	Ⓩ	

7 TEST BOOK SERIAL NUMBER
(Copy from front of test book.)

0	0	0	0	0	0
1	1	1	1	1	1
2	2	2	2	2	2
3	3	3	3	3	3
4	4	4	4	4	4
5	5	5	5	5	5
6	6	6	6	6	6
7	7	7	7	7	7
8	8	8	8	8	8
9	9	9	9	9	9

9 BOOK ID
(Copy from back of test book.)

Quality Assurance Mark ●

Chemistry *Fill in circle CE only if II is correct explanation of I.

	I	II	CE*		I	II	CE*
101	T F	T F	○	109	T F	T F	○
102	T F	T F	○	110	T F	T F	○
103	T F	T F	○	111	T F	T F	○
104	T F	T F	○	112	T F	T F	○
105	T F	T F	○	113	T F	T F	○
106	T F	T F	○	114	T F	T F	○
107	T F	T F	○	115	T F	T F	○
108	T F	T F	○				

FOR OFFICIAL USE ONLY				
R/C	W/S1	FS/S2	CS/S3	WS

PLEASE DO NOT WRITE IN THIS AREA   ○○○○○○○○○○○○○○○○○○○○○○○○○○○○○○   **SERIAL #**

23459 College Board 15b-10820-Text

SAT Subject Tests™

COMPLETE MARK ● **EXAMPLES OF INCOMPLETE MARKS** Ⓐ ⊗ ⊖ Ⓓ ⊘ ⊘ ⊛

You must use a No. 2 pencil and marks must be complete. Do not use a mechanical pencil. It is very important that you fill in the entire circle darkly and completely. If you change your response, erase as completely as possible. Incomplete marks or erasures may affect your score.

1 **Your Name:**
(Print)

Last _____ First _____ M.I. _____

I agree to the conditions on the front and back of the SAT Subject Tests™ book. I also agree with the SAT Test Security and Fairness policies and understand that any violation of these policies will result in score cancellation and may result in reporting of certain violations to law enforcement.

Signature: _____ Today's Date: ___ / ___ / ___
                                                  MM   DD   YY

Home Address: _____
(Print) Number and Street   City   State/Country   Zip Code

Phone: (____) _____ Test Center: _____
                              (Print)   City   State/Country

2 **YOUR NAME**
Last Name (First 6 Letters) First Name (First 4 Letters) Mid. Init.

3 **DATE OF BIRTH**
MONTH | DAY | YEAR
○ Jan
○ Feb
○ Mar
○ Apr
○ May
○ Jun
○ Jul
○ Aug
○ Sep
○ Oct
○ Nov
○ Dec

4 **REGISTRATION NUMBER**
(Copy from Admission Ticket.)

5 **ZIP CODE**

6 **TEST CENTER**
(Supplied by Test Center Supervisor.)

Important: Fill in items 8 and 9 exactly as shown on the back of test book.

7 **TEST BOOK SERIAL NUMBER**
(Copy from front of test book.)

8 **BOOK CODE**
(Copy and grid as on back of test book.)

9 **BOOK ID**
(Copy from back of test book.)

PLEASE MAKE SURE to fill in these fields completely and correctly. If they are not correct, we won't be able to score your test(s)!

FOR OFFICIAL USE ONLY
⓪①②③④⑤⑥
⓪①②③④⑤⑥
⓪①②③④⑤⑥

103648-77191 • NS1114C1085 • Printed in U.S.A.

© 2015 The College Board. College Board, SAT, and the acorn logo are registered trademarks of the College Board. SAT Subject Tests is a trademark owned by the College Board.

194415-001   1 2 3 4 5 A B C D E   Printed in the USA   ISD11312

783175

PLEASE DO NOT WRITE IN THIS AREA

SERIAL #

23459 College Board 15b-10820-Text

You must use a No. 2 pencil and marks must be complete. Do not use a mechanical pencil. It is very important that you fill in the entire circle darkly and completely. If you change your response, erase as completely as possible. Incomplete marks or erasures may affect your score.

- ○ Literature
- ○ Biology E
- ○ Biology M
- ○ Chemistry
- ○ Physics
- ○ Mathematics Level 1
- ○ Mathematics Level 2
- ○ U.S. History
- ○ World History
- ○ French
- ○ German
- ○ Italian
- ○ Latin
- ○ Modern Hebrew
- ○ Spanish
- ○ Chinese Listening
- ○ French Listening
- ○ German Listening
- ○ Japanese Listening
- ○ Korean Listening
- ○ Spanish Listening

Background Questions: ① ② ③ ④ ⑤ ⑥ ⑦ ⑧ ⑨

PLEASE MAKE SURE to fill in these fields completely and correctly. If they are not correct, we won't be able to score your test(s)!

(Answer grid, questions 1–100, each with options A B C D E)

1–25 | 26–50 | 51–75 | 76–100

7 TEST BOOK SERIAL NUMBER (Copy from front of test book.)

8 BOOK CODE (Copy and grid as on back of test book.)

9 BOOK ID (Copy from back of test book.)

Quality Assurance Mark

Chemistry *Fill in circle CE only if II is correct explanation of I.

	I	II	CE*		I	II	CE*
101	T F	T F	○	109	T F	T F	○
102	T F	T F	○	110	T F	T F	○
103	T F	T F	○	111	T F	T F	○
104	T F	T F	○	112	T F	T F	○
105	T F	T F	○	113	T F	T F	○
106	T F	T F	○	114	T F	T F	○
107	T F	T F	○	115	T F	T F	○
108	T F	T F	○				

FOR OFFICIAL USE ONLY

R/C	W/S1	FS/S2	CS/S3	WS

CERTIFICATION STATEMENT

Copy the statement below and sign your name as you would an official document.

I hereby agree to the conditions set forth online at sat.collegeboard.org and in any paper registration materials given to me and certify that I am the person whose name, address and signature appear on this answer sheet.

Signature _____ Date _____

23459 College Board 15b-10820-Text

○ Literature
○ Biology E
○ Biology M
○ Chemistry
○ Physics

○ Mathematics Level 1
○ Mathematics Level 2
○ U.S. History
○ World History
○ French

○ German
○ Italian
○ Latin
○ Modern Hebrew
○ Spanish

○ Chinese Listening
○ French Listening
○ German Listening

○ Japanese Listening
○ Korean Listening
○ Spanish Listening

Background Questions: ① ② ③ ④ ⑤ ⑥ ⑦ ⑧ ⑨

PLEASE MAKE SURE to fill in these fields completely and correctly. If they are not correct, we won't be able to score your test(s)!

Questions 1–100: each row has answer options A B C D E

Quality Assurance Mark ●

7 TEST BOOK SERIAL NUMBER (Copy from front of test book.)

digits 0–9

8 BOOK CODE (Copy and grid as on back of test book.)

0 A 0
1 B 1
2 C 2
3 D 3
4 E 4
5 F 5
6 G 6
7 H 7
8 I 8
9 J 9
K
L
M
N
O
P
Q
R
S
T
U
V
W
X
Y
Z

9 BOOK ID (Copy from back of test book.)

Chemistry *Fill in circle CE only if II is correct explanation of I.

	I	II	CE*		I	II	CE*
101	T F	T F	○	109	T F	T F	○
102	T F	T F	○	110	T F	T F	○
103	T F	T F	○	111	T F	T F	○
104	T F	T F	○	112	T F	T F	○
105	T F	T F	○	113	T F	T F	○
106	T F	T F	○	114	T F	T F	○
107	T F	T F	○	115	T F	T F	○
108	T F	T F	○				

FOR OFFICIAL USE ONLY				
R/C	W/S1	FS/S2	CS/S3	WS

Page 3

COMPLETE MARK ●   EXAMPLES OF INCOMPLETE MARKS Ⓐ ⊗ ⊕ Ⓒ / Ⓒ Ⓒ

You must use a No. 2 pencil and marks must be complete. Do not use a mechanical pencil. It is very important that you fill in the entire circle darkly and completely. If you change your response, erase as completely as possible. Incomplete marks or erasures may affect your score.

○ Literature
○ Biology E
○ Biology M
○ Chemistry
○ Physics

○ Mathematics Level 1
○ Mathematics Level 2
○ U.S. History
○ World History
○ French

○ German
○ Italian
○ Latin
○ Modern Hebrew
○ Spanish

○ Chinese Listening
○ French Listening
○ German Listening

○ Japanese Listening
○ Korean Listening
○ Spanish Listening

Background Questions: ① ② ③ ④ ⑤ ⑥ ⑦ ⑧ ⑨

PLEASE MAKE SURE to fill in these fields completely and correctly. If they are not correct, we won't be able to score your test(s)!

#		#		#		#	
1	Ⓐ Ⓑ Ⓒ Ⓓ Ⓔ	26	Ⓐ Ⓑ Ⓒ Ⓓ Ⓔ	51	Ⓐ Ⓑ Ⓒ Ⓓ Ⓔ	76	Ⓐ Ⓑ Ⓒ Ⓓ Ⓔ
2	Ⓐ Ⓑ Ⓒ Ⓓ Ⓔ	27	Ⓐ Ⓑ Ⓒ Ⓓ Ⓔ	52	Ⓐ Ⓑ Ⓒ Ⓓ Ⓔ	77	Ⓐ Ⓑ Ⓒ Ⓓ Ⓔ
3	Ⓐ Ⓑ Ⓒ Ⓓ Ⓔ	28	Ⓐ Ⓑ Ⓒ Ⓓ Ⓔ	53	Ⓐ Ⓑ Ⓒ Ⓓ Ⓔ	78	Ⓐ Ⓑ Ⓒ Ⓓ Ⓔ
4	Ⓐ Ⓑ Ⓒ Ⓓ Ⓔ	29	Ⓐ Ⓑ Ⓒ Ⓓ Ⓔ	54	Ⓐ Ⓑ Ⓒ Ⓓ Ⓔ	79	Ⓐ Ⓑ Ⓒ Ⓓ Ⓔ
5	Ⓐ Ⓑ Ⓒ Ⓓ Ⓔ	30	Ⓐ Ⓑ Ⓒ Ⓓ Ⓔ	55	Ⓐ Ⓑ Ⓒ Ⓓ Ⓔ	80	Ⓐ Ⓑ Ⓒ Ⓓ Ⓔ
6	Ⓐ Ⓑ Ⓒ Ⓓ Ⓔ	31	Ⓐ Ⓑ Ⓒ Ⓓ Ⓔ	56	Ⓐ Ⓑ Ⓒ Ⓓ Ⓔ	81	Ⓐ Ⓑ Ⓒ Ⓓ Ⓔ
7	Ⓐ Ⓑ Ⓒ Ⓓ Ⓔ	32	Ⓐ Ⓑ Ⓒ Ⓓ Ⓔ	57	Ⓐ Ⓑ Ⓒ Ⓓ Ⓔ	82	Ⓐ Ⓑ Ⓒ Ⓓ Ⓔ
8	Ⓐ Ⓑ Ⓒ Ⓓ Ⓔ	33	Ⓐ Ⓑ Ⓒ Ⓓ Ⓔ	58	Ⓐ Ⓑ Ⓒ Ⓓ Ⓔ	83	Ⓐ Ⓑ Ⓒ Ⓓ Ⓔ
9	Ⓐ Ⓑ Ⓒ Ⓓ Ⓔ	34	Ⓐ Ⓑ Ⓒ Ⓓ Ⓔ	59	Ⓐ Ⓑ Ⓒ Ⓓ Ⓔ	84	Ⓐ Ⓑ Ⓒ Ⓓ Ⓔ
10	Ⓐ Ⓑ Ⓒ Ⓓ Ⓔ	35	Ⓐ Ⓑ Ⓒ Ⓓ Ⓔ	60	Ⓐ Ⓑ Ⓒ Ⓓ Ⓔ	85	Ⓐ Ⓑ Ⓒ Ⓓ Ⓔ
11	Ⓐ Ⓑ Ⓒ Ⓓ Ⓔ	36	Ⓐ Ⓑ Ⓒ Ⓓ Ⓔ	61	Ⓐ Ⓑ Ⓒ Ⓓ Ⓔ	86	Ⓐ Ⓑ Ⓒ Ⓓ Ⓔ
12	Ⓐ Ⓑ Ⓒ Ⓓ Ⓔ	37	Ⓐ Ⓑ Ⓒ Ⓓ Ⓔ	62	Ⓐ Ⓑ Ⓒ Ⓓ Ⓔ	87	Ⓐ Ⓑ Ⓒ Ⓓ Ⓔ
13	Ⓐ Ⓑ Ⓒ Ⓓ Ⓔ	38	Ⓐ Ⓑ Ⓒ Ⓓ Ⓔ	63	Ⓐ Ⓑ Ⓒ Ⓓ Ⓔ	88	Ⓐ Ⓑ Ⓒ Ⓓ Ⓔ
14	Ⓐ Ⓑ Ⓒ Ⓓ Ⓔ	39	Ⓐ Ⓑ Ⓒ Ⓓ Ⓔ	64	Ⓐ Ⓑ Ⓒ Ⓓ Ⓔ	89	Ⓐ Ⓑ Ⓒ Ⓓ Ⓔ
15	Ⓐ Ⓑ Ⓒ Ⓓ Ⓔ	40	Ⓐ Ⓑ Ⓒ Ⓓ Ⓔ	65	Ⓐ Ⓑ Ⓒ Ⓓ Ⓔ	90	Ⓐ Ⓑ Ⓒ Ⓓ Ⓔ
16	Ⓐ Ⓑ Ⓒ Ⓓ Ⓔ	41	Ⓐ Ⓑ Ⓒ Ⓓ Ⓔ	66	Ⓐ Ⓑ Ⓒ Ⓓ Ⓔ	91	Ⓐ Ⓑ Ⓒ Ⓓ Ⓔ
17	Ⓐ Ⓑ Ⓒ Ⓓ Ⓔ	42	Ⓐ Ⓑ Ⓒ Ⓓ Ⓔ	67	Ⓐ Ⓑ Ⓒ Ⓓ Ⓔ	92	Ⓐ Ⓑ Ⓒ Ⓓ Ⓔ
18	Ⓐ Ⓑ Ⓒ Ⓓ Ⓔ	43	Ⓐ Ⓑ Ⓒ Ⓓ Ⓔ	68	Ⓐ Ⓑ Ⓒ Ⓓ Ⓔ	93	Ⓐ Ⓑ Ⓒ Ⓓ Ⓔ
19	Ⓐ Ⓑ Ⓒ Ⓓ Ⓔ	44	Ⓐ Ⓑ Ⓒ Ⓓ Ⓔ	69	Ⓐ Ⓑ Ⓒ Ⓓ Ⓔ	94	Ⓐ Ⓑ Ⓒ Ⓓ Ⓔ
20	Ⓐ Ⓑ Ⓒ Ⓓ Ⓔ	45	Ⓐ Ⓑ Ⓒ Ⓓ Ⓔ	70	Ⓐ Ⓑ Ⓒ Ⓓ Ⓔ	95	Ⓐ Ⓑ Ⓒ Ⓓ Ⓔ
21	Ⓐ Ⓑ Ⓒ Ⓓ Ⓔ	46	Ⓐ Ⓑ Ⓒ Ⓓ Ⓔ	71	Ⓐ Ⓑ Ⓒ Ⓓ Ⓔ	96	Ⓐ Ⓑ Ⓒ Ⓓ Ⓔ
22	Ⓐ Ⓑ Ⓒ Ⓓ Ⓔ	47	Ⓐ Ⓑ Ⓒ Ⓓ Ⓔ	72	Ⓐ Ⓑ Ⓒ Ⓓ Ⓔ	97	Ⓐ Ⓑ Ⓒ Ⓓ Ⓔ
23	Ⓐ Ⓑ Ⓒ Ⓓ Ⓔ	48	Ⓐ Ⓑ Ⓒ Ⓓ Ⓔ	73	Ⓐ Ⓑ Ⓒ Ⓓ Ⓔ	98	Ⓐ Ⓑ Ⓒ Ⓓ Ⓔ
24	Ⓐ Ⓑ Ⓒ Ⓓ Ⓔ	49	Ⓐ Ⓑ Ⓒ Ⓓ Ⓔ	74	Ⓐ Ⓑ Ⓒ Ⓓ Ⓔ	99	Ⓐ Ⓑ Ⓒ Ⓓ Ⓔ
25	Ⓐ Ⓑ Ⓒ Ⓓ Ⓔ	50	Ⓐ Ⓑ Ⓒ Ⓓ Ⓔ	75	Ⓐ Ⓑ Ⓒ Ⓓ Ⓔ	100	Ⓐ Ⓑ Ⓒ Ⓓ Ⓔ

Chemistry *Fill in circle CE only if II is correct explanation of I.

	I	II	CE*		I	II	CE*
101	Ⓣ Ⓕ	Ⓣ Ⓕ	○	109	Ⓣ Ⓕ	Ⓣ Ⓕ	○
102	Ⓣ Ⓕ	Ⓣ Ⓕ	○	110	Ⓣ Ⓕ	Ⓣ Ⓕ	○
103	Ⓣ Ⓕ	Ⓣ Ⓕ	○	111	Ⓣ Ⓕ	Ⓣ Ⓕ	○
104	Ⓣ Ⓕ	Ⓣ Ⓕ	○	112	Ⓣ Ⓕ	Ⓣ Ⓕ	○
105	Ⓣ Ⓕ	Ⓣ Ⓕ	○	113	Ⓣ Ⓕ	Ⓣ Ⓕ	○
106	Ⓣ Ⓕ	Ⓣ Ⓕ	○	114	Ⓣ Ⓕ	Ⓣ Ⓕ	○
107	Ⓣ Ⓕ	Ⓣ Ⓕ	○	115	Ⓣ Ⓕ	Ⓣ Ⓕ	○
108	Ⓣ Ⓕ	Ⓣ Ⓕ	○				

FOR OFFICIAL USE ONLY

R/C	W/S1	FS/S2	CS/S3	WS

8 BOOK CODE
(Copy and grid as on back of test book.)

| 0 A 0 |
| 1 B 1 |
| 2 C 2 |
| 3 D 3 |
| 4 E 4 |
| 5 F 5 |
| 6 G 6 |
| 7 H 7 |
| 8 I 8 |
| 9 J 9 |
| K |
| L |
| M |
| N |
| O |
| P |
| Q |
| R |
| S |
| T |
| U |
| V |
| W |
| X |
| Y |
| Z |

7 TEST BOOK SERIAL NUMBER
(Copy from front of test book.)

0	0	0	0	0	0
1	1	1	1	1	1
2	2	2	2	2	2
3	3	3	3	3	3
4	4	4	4	4	4
5	5	5	5	5	5
6	6	6	6	6	6
7	7	7	7	7	7
8	8	8	8	8	8
9	9	9	9	9	9

9 BOOK ID
(Copy from back of test book.)

Quality Assurance Mark ●

Page 4

PLEASE DO NOT WRITE IN THIS AREA

○○○○○○○○○○○○○○○○○○○○○○○○○○○○○○

SERIAL #

23459 College Board 15b-10820-Text

SAT Subject Tests™

You must use a No. 2 pencil and marks must be complete. Do not use a mechanical pencil. It is very important that you fill in the entire circle darkly and completely. If you change your response, erase as completely as possible. Incomplete marks or erasures may affect your score.

1 Your Name:
(Print)

Last   First   M.I.

I agree to the conditions on the front and back of the SAT Subject Tests™ book. I also agree with the SAT Test Security and Fairness policies and understand that any violation of these policies will result in score cancellation and may result in reporting of certain violations to law enforcement.

Signature: _____

Today's Date: ___ / ___ / ___
MM   DD   YY

Home Address: _____
(Print)   Number and Street   City   State/Country   Zip Code

Phone: ( )   Test Center: _____
(Print)   City   State/Country

2 YOUR NAME

Last Name (First 6 Letters) | First Name (First 4 Letters) | Mid. Init.

3 DATE OF BIRTH

MONTH | DAY | YEAR

○ Jan
○ Feb
○ Mar
○ Apr
○ May
○ Jun
○ Jul
○ Aug
○ Sep
○ Oct
○ Nov
○ Dec

4 REGISTRATION NUMBER
(Copy from Admission Ticket.)

Important:
Fill in items 8 and 9 exactly as shown on the back of test book.

7 TEST BOOK SERIAL NUMBER
(Copy from front of test book.)

8 BOOK CODE
(Copy and grid as on back of test book.)

9 BOOK ID
(Copy from back of test book.)

PLEASE MAKE SURE to fill in these fields completely and correctly. If they are not correct, we won't be able to score your test(s)!

5 ZIP CODE

6 TEST CENTER
(Supplied by Test Center Supervisor.)

FOR OFFICIAL USE ONLY
0 1 2 3 4 5 6
0 1 2 3 4 5 6
0 1 2 3 4 5 6

103648-77191 · NS1114C1085 · Printed in U.S.A.

194415-001   1 2 3 4 5 A B C D E   Printed in the USA   ISD11312   783175

PLEASE DO NOT WRITE IN THIS AREA   **SERIAL #**

○ Literature
○ Biology E
○ Biology M
○ Chemistry
○ Physics

○ Mathematics Level 1
○ Mathematics Level 2
○ U.S. History
○ World History
○ French

○ German
○ Italian
○ Latin
○ Modern Hebrew
○ Spanish

○ Chinese Listening
○ French Listening
○ German Listening

○ Japanese Listening
○ Korean Listening
○ Spanish Listening

Background Questions: ① ② ③ ④ ⑤ ⑥ ⑦ ⑧ ⑨

1 Ⓐ Ⓑ Ⓒ Ⓓ Ⓔ   26 Ⓐ Ⓑ Ⓒ Ⓓ Ⓔ   51 Ⓐ Ⓑ Ⓒ Ⓓ Ⓔ   76 Ⓐ Ⓑ Ⓒ Ⓓ Ⓔ
2 Ⓐ Ⓑ Ⓒ Ⓓ Ⓔ   27 Ⓐ Ⓑ Ⓒ Ⓓ Ⓔ   52 Ⓐ Ⓑ Ⓒ Ⓓ Ⓔ   77 Ⓐ Ⓑ Ⓒ Ⓓ Ⓔ
3 Ⓐ Ⓑ Ⓒ Ⓓ Ⓔ   28 Ⓐ Ⓑ Ⓒ Ⓓ Ⓔ   53 Ⓐ Ⓑ Ⓒ Ⓓ Ⓔ   78 Ⓐ Ⓑ Ⓒ Ⓓ Ⓔ
4 Ⓐ Ⓑ Ⓒ Ⓓ Ⓔ   29 Ⓐ Ⓑ Ⓒ Ⓓ Ⓔ   54 Ⓐ Ⓑ Ⓒ Ⓓ Ⓔ   79 Ⓐ Ⓑ Ⓒ Ⓓ Ⓔ
5 Ⓐ Ⓑ Ⓒ Ⓓ Ⓔ   30 Ⓐ Ⓑ Ⓒ Ⓓ Ⓔ   55 Ⓐ Ⓑ Ⓒ Ⓓ Ⓔ   80 Ⓐ Ⓑ Ⓒ Ⓓ Ⓔ
6 Ⓐ Ⓑ Ⓒ Ⓓ Ⓔ   31 Ⓐ Ⓑ Ⓒ Ⓓ Ⓔ   56 Ⓐ Ⓑ Ⓒ Ⓓ Ⓔ   81 Ⓐ Ⓑ Ⓒ Ⓓ Ⓔ
7 Ⓐ Ⓑ Ⓒ Ⓓ Ⓔ   32 Ⓐ Ⓑ Ⓒ Ⓓ Ⓔ   57 Ⓐ Ⓑ Ⓒ Ⓓ Ⓔ   82 Ⓐ Ⓑ Ⓒ Ⓓ Ⓔ
8 Ⓐ Ⓑ Ⓒ Ⓓ Ⓔ   33 Ⓐ Ⓑ Ⓒ Ⓓ Ⓔ   58 Ⓐ Ⓑ Ⓒ Ⓓ Ⓔ   83 Ⓐ Ⓑ Ⓒ Ⓓ Ⓔ
9 Ⓐ Ⓑ Ⓒ Ⓓ Ⓔ   34 Ⓐ Ⓑ Ⓒ Ⓓ Ⓔ   59 Ⓐ Ⓑ Ⓒ Ⓓ Ⓔ   84 Ⓐ Ⓑ Ⓒ Ⓓ Ⓔ
10 Ⓐ Ⓑ Ⓒ Ⓓ Ⓔ   35 Ⓐ Ⓑ Ⓒ Ⓓ Ⓔ   60 Ⓐ Ⓑ Ⓒ Ⓓ Ⓔ   85 Ⓐ Ⓑ Ⓒ Ⓓ Ⓔ
11 Ⓐ Ⓑ Ⓒ Ⓓ Ⓔ   36 Ⓐ Ⓑ Ⓒ Ⓓ Ⓔ   61 Ⓐ Ⓑ Ⓒ Ⓓ Ⓔ   86 Ⓐ Ⓑ Ⓒ Ⓓ Ⓔ
12 Ⓐ Ⓑ Ⓒ Ⓓ Ⓔ   37 Ⓐ Ⓑ Ⓒ Ⓓ Ⓔ   62 Ⓐ Ⓑ Ⓒ Ⓓ Ⓔ   87 Ⓐ Ⓑ Ⓒ Ⓓ Ⓔ
13 Ⓐ Ⓑ Ⓒ Ⓓ Ⓔ   38 Ⓐ Ⓑ Ⓒ Ⓓ Ⓔ   63 Ⓐ Ⓑ Ⓒ Ⓓ Ⓔ   88 Ⓐ Ⓑ Ⓒ Ⓓ Ⓔ
14 Ⓐ Ⓑ Ⓒ Ⓓ Ⓔ   39 Ⓐ Ⓑ Ⓒ Ⓓ Ⓔ   64 Ⓐ Ⓑ Ⓒ Ⓓ Ⓔ   89 Ⓐ Ⓑ Ⓒ Ⓓ Ⓔ
15 Ⓐ Ⓑ Ⓒ Ⓓ Ⓔ   40 Ⓐ Ⓑ Ⓒ Ⓓ Ⓔ   65 Ⓐ Ⓑ Ⓒ Ⓓ Ⓔ   90 Ⓐ Ⓑ Ⓒ Ⓓ Ⓔ
16 Ⓐ Ⓑ Ⓒ Ⓓ Ⓔ   41 Ⓐ Ⓑ Ⓒ Ⓓ Ⓔ   66 Ⓐ Ⓑ Ⓒ Ⓓ Ⓔ   91 Ⓐ Ⓑ Ⓒ Ⓓ Ⓔ
17 Ⓐ Ⓑ Ⓒ Ⓓ Ⓔ   42 Ⓐ Ⓑ Ⓒ Ⓓ Ⓔ   67 Ⓐ Ⓑ Ⓒ Ⓓ Ⓔ   92 Ⓐ Ⓑ Ⓒ Ⓓ Ⓔ
18 Ⓐ Ⓑ Ⓒ Ⓓ Ⓔ   43 Ⓐ Ⓑ Ⓒ Ⓓ Ⓔ   68 Ⓐ Ⓑ Ⓒ Ⓓ Ⓔ   93 Ⓐ Ⓑ Ⓒ Ⓓ Ⓔ
19 Ⓐ Ⓑ Ⓒ Ⓓ Ⓔ   44 Ⓐ Ⓑ Ⓒ Ⓓ Ⓔ   69 Ⓐ Ⓑ Ⓒ Ⓓ Ⓔ   94 Ⓐ Ⓑ Ⓒ Ⓓ Ⓔ
20 Ⓐ Ⓑ Ⓒ Ⓓ Ⓔ   45 Ⓐ Ⓑ Ⓒ Ⓓ Ⓔ   70 Ⓐ Ⓑ Ⓒ Ⓓ Ⓔ   95 Ⓐ Ⓑ Ⓒ Ⓓ Ⓔ
21 Ⓐ Ⓑ Ⓒ Ⓓ Ⓔ   46 Ⓐ Ⓑ Ⓒ Ⓓ Ⓔ   71 Ⓐ Ⓑ Ⓒ Ⓓ Ⓔ   96 Ⓐ Ⓑ Ⓒ Ⓓ Ⓔ
22 Ⓐ Ⓑ Ⓒ Ⓓ Ⓔ   47 Ⓐ Ⓑ Ⓒ Ⓓ Ⓔ   72 Ⓐ Ⓑ Ⓒ Ⓓ Ⓔ   97 Ⓐ Ⓑ Ⓒ Ⓓ Ⓔ
23 Ⓐ Ⓑ Ⓒ Ⓓ Ⓔ   48 Ⓐ Ⓑ Ⓒ Ⓓ Ⓔ   73 Ⓐ Ⓑ Ⓒ Ⓓ Ⓔ   98 Ⓐ Ⓑ Ⓒ Ⓓ Ⓔ
24 Ⓐ Ⓑ Ⓒ Ⓓ Ⓔ   49 Ⓐ Ⓑ Ⓒ Ⓓ Ⓔ   74 Ⓐ Ⓑ Ⓒ Ⓓ Ⓔ   99 Ⓐ Ⓑ Ⓒ Ⓓ Ⓔ
25 Ⓐ Ⓑ Ⓒ Ⓓ Ⓔ   50 Ⓐ Ⓑ Ⓒ Ⓓ Ⓔ   75 Ⓐ Ⓑ Ⓒ Ⓓ Ⓔ   100 Ⓐ Ⓑ Ⓒ Ⓓ Ⓔ

PLEASE MAKE SURE to fill in these fields completely and correctly. If they are not correct, we won't be able to score your test(s)!

8 BOOK CODE
(Copy and grid as on back of test book.)

0 Ⓐ 0
1 Ⓑ 1
2 Ⓒ 2
3 Ⓓ 3
4 Ⓔ 4
5 Ⓕ 5
6 Ⓖ 6
7 Ⓗ 7
8 Ⓘ 8
9 Ⓙ 9
Ⓚ
Ⓛ
Ⓜ
Ⓝ
Ⓞ
Ⓟ
Ⓠ
Ⓡ
Ⓢ
Ⓣ
Ⓤ
Ⓥ
Ⓦ
Ⓧ
Ⓨ
Ⓩ

7 TEST BOOK SERIAL NUMBER
(Copy from front of test book.)

0 0 0 0 0 0
1 1 1 1 1 1
2 2 2 2 2 2
3 3 3 3 3 3
4 4 4 4 4 4
5 5 5 5 5 5
6 6 6 6 6 6
7 7 7 7 7 7
8 8 8 8 8 8
9 9 9 9 9 9

9 BOOK ID
(Copy from back of test book.)

Quality Assurance Mark ●

Chemistry *Fill in circle CE only if II is correct explanation of I.

	I	II	CE*		I	II	CE*
101	T F	T F	○	109	T F	T F	○
102	T F	T F	○	110	T F	T F	○
103	T F	T F	○	111	T F	T F	○
104	T F	T F	○	112	T F	T F	○
105	T F	T F	○	113	T F	T F	○
106	T F	T F	○	114	T F	T F	○
107	T F	T F	○	115	T F	T F	○
108	T F	T F	○				

FOR OFFICIAL USE ONLY				
R/C	W/S1	FS/S2	CS/S3	WS

CERTIFICATION STATEMENT Copy the statement below and sign your name as you would an official document.

I hereby agree to the conditions set forth online at sat.collegeboard.org and in any paper registration materials given to me and certify that I am the person whose name, address and signature appear on this answer sheet.

_____

_____

_____

_____

Signature _____   Date _____

- ○ Literature
- ○ Biology E
- ○ Biology M
- ○ Chemistry
- ○ Physics

- ○ Mathematics Level 1
- ○ Mathematics Level 2
- ○ U.S. History
- ○ World History
- ○ French

- ○ German
- ○ Italian
- ○ Latin
- ○ Modern Hebrew
- ○ Spanish

- ○ Chinese Listening
- ○ French Listening
- ○ German Listening

- ○ Japanese Listening
- ○ Korean Listening
- ○ Spanish Listening

Background Questions: ① ② ③ ④ ⑤ ⑥ ⑦ ⑧ ⑨

PLEASE MAKE SURE to fill in these fields completely and correctly. If they are not correct, we won't be able to score your test(s)!

Quality Assurance Mark ●

Chemistry *Fill in circle CE only if II is correct explanation of I.

	I	II	CE*		I	II	CE*
101	Ⓣ Ⓕ	Ⓣ Ⓕ	○	109	Ⓣ Ⓕ	Ⓣ Ⓕ	○
102	Ⓣ Ⓕ	Ⓣ Ⓕ	○	110	Ⓣ Ⓕ	Ⓣ Ⓕ	○
103	Ⓣ Ⓕ	Ⓣ Ⓕ	○	111	Ⓣ Ⓕ	Ⓣ Ⓕ	○
104	Ⓣ Ⓕ	Ⓣ Ⓕ	○	112	Ⓣ Ⓕ	Ⓣ Ⓕ	○
105	Ⓣ Ⓕ	Ⓣ Ⓕ	○	113	Ⓣ Ⓕ	Ⓣ Ⓕ	○
106	Ⓣ Ⓕ	Ⓣ Ⓕ	○	114	Ⓣ Ⓕ	Ⓣ Ⓕ	○
107	Ⓣ Ⓕ	Ⓣ Ⓕ	○	115	Ⓣ Ⓕ	Ⓣ Ⓕ	○
108	Ⓣ Ⓕ	Ⓣ Ⓕ	○				

7 TEST BOOK SERIAL NUMBER (Copy from front of test book.)

8 BOOK CODE (Copy and grid as on back of test book.)

9 BOOK ID (Copy from back of test book.)

FOR OFFICIAL USE ONLY				
R/C	W/S1	FS/S2	CS/S3	WS

○ Literature
○ Biology E
○ Biology M
○ Chemistry
○ Physics

○ Mathematics Level 1
○ Mathematics Level 2
○ U.S. History
○ World History
○ French

○ German
○ Italian
○ Latin
○ Modern Hebrew
○ Spanish

○ Chinese Listening
○ French Listening
○ German Listening

○ Japanese Listening
○ Korean Listening
○ Spanish Listening

Background Questions: ① ② ③ ④ ⑤ ⑥ ⑦ ⑧ ⑨

PLEASE MAKE SURE to fill in these fields completely and correctly. If they are not correct, we won't be able to score your test(s)!

1 Ⓐ Ⓑ Ⓒ Ⓓ Ⓔ   26 Ⓐ Ⓑ Ⓒ Ⓓ Ⓔ   51 Ⓐ Ⓑ Ⓒ Ⓓ Ⓔ   76 Ⓐ Ⓑ Ⓒ Ⓓ Ⓔ
2 Ⓐ Ⓑ Ⓒ Ⓓ Ⓔ   27 Ⓐ Ⓑ Ⓒ Ⓓ Ⓔ   52 Ⓐ Ⓑ Ⓒ Ⓓ Ⓔ   77 Ⓐ Ⓑ Ⓒ Ⓓ Ⓔ
3 Ⓐ Ⓑ Ⓒ Ⓓ Ⓔ   28 Ⓐ Ⓑ Ⓒ Ⓓ Ⓔ   53 Ⓐ Ⓑ Ⓒ Ⓓ Ⓔ   78 Ⓐ Ⓑ Ⓒ Ⓓ Ⓔ
4 Ⓐ Ⓑ Ⓒ Ⓓ Ⓔ   29 Ⓐ Ⓑ Ⓒ Ⓓ Ⓔ   54 Ⓐ Ⓑ Ⓒ Ⓓ Ⓔ   79 Ⓐ Ⓑ Ⓒ Ⓓ Ⓔ
5 Ⓐ Ⓑ Ⓒ Ⓓ Ⓔ   30 Ⓐ Ⓑ Ⓒ Ⓓ Ⓔ   55 Ⓐ Ⓑ Ⓒ Ⓓ Ⓔ   80 Ⓐ Ⓑ Ⓒ Ⓓ Ⓔ
6 Ⓐ Ⓑ Ⓒ Ⓓ Ⓔ   31 Ⓐ Ⓑ Ⓒ Ⓓ Ⓔ   56 Ⓐ Ⓑ Ⓒ Ⓓ Ⓔ   81 Ⓐ Ⓑ Ⓒ Ⓓ Ⓔ
7 Ⓐ Ⓑ Ⓒ Ⓓ Ⓔ   32 Ⓐ Ⓑ Ⓒ Ⓓ Ⓔ   57 Ⓐ Ⓑ Ⓒ Ⓓ Ⓔ   82 Ⓐ Ⓑ Ⓒ Ⓓ Ⓔ
8 Ⓐ Ⓑ Ⓒ Ⓓ Ⓔ   33 Ⓐ Ⓑ Ⓒ Ⓓ Ⓔ   58 Ⓐ Ⓑ Ⓒ Ⓓ Ⓔ   83 Ⓐ Ⓑ Ⓒ Ⓓ Ⓔ
9 Ⓐ Ⓑ Ⓒ Ⓓ Ⓔ   34 Ⓐ Ⓑ Ⓒ Ⓓ Ⓔ   59 Ⓐ Ⓑ Ⓒ Ⓓ Ⓔ   84 Ⓐ Ⓑ Ⓒ Ⓓ Ⓔ
10 Ⓐ Ⓑ Ⓒ Ⓓ Ⓔ   35 Ⓐ Ⓑ Ⓒ Ⓓ Ⓔ   60 Ⓐ Ⓑ Ⓒ Ⓓ Ⓔ   85 Ⓐ Ⓑ Ⓒ Ⓓ Ⓔ
11 Ⓐ Ⓑ Ⓒ Ⓓ Ⓔ   36 Ⓐ Ⓑ Ⓒ Ⓓ Ⓔ   61 Ⓐ Ⓑ Ⓒ Ⓓ Ⓔ   86 Ⓐ Ⓑ Ⓒ Ⓓ Ⓔ
12 Ⓐ Ⓑ Ⓒ Ⓓ Ⓔ   37 Ⓐ Ⓑ Ⓒ Ⓓ Ⓔ   62 Ⓐ Ⓑ Ⓒ Ⓓ Ⓔ   87 Ⓐ Ⓑ Ⓒ Ⓓ Ⓔ
13 Ⓐ Ⓑ Ⓒ Ⓓ Ⓔ   38 Ⓐ Ⓑ Ⓒ Ⓓ Ⓔ   63 Ⓐ Ⓑ Ⓒ Ⓓ Ⓔ   88 Ⓐ Ⓑ Ⓒ Ⓓ Ⓔ
14 Ⓐ Ⓑ Ⓒ Ⓓ Ⓔ   39 Ⓐ Ⓑ Ⓒ Ⓓ Ⓔ   64 Ⓐ Ⓑ Ⓒ Ⓓ Ⓔ   89 Ⓐ Ⓑ Ⓒ Ⓓ Ⓔ
15 Ⓐ Ⓑ Ⓒ Ⓓ Ⓔ   40 Ⓐ Ⓑ Ⓒ Ⓓ Ⓔ   65 Ⓐ Ⓑ Ⓒ Ⓓ Ⓔ   90 Ⓐ Ⓑ Ⓒ Ⓓ Ⓔ
16 Ⓐ Ⓑ Ⓒ Ⓓ Ⓔ   41 Ⓐ Ⓑ Ⓒ Ⓓ Ⓔ   66 Ⓐ Ⓑ Ⓒ Ⓓ Ⓔ   91 Ⓐ Ⓑ Ⓒ Ⓓ Ⓔ
17 Ⓐ Ⓑ Ⓒ Ⓓ Ⓔ   42 Ⓐ Ⓑ Ⓒ Ⓓ Ⓔ   67 Ⓐ Ⓑ Ⓒ Ⓓ Ⓔ   92 Ⓐ Ⓑ Ⓒ Ⓓ Ⓔ
18 Ⓐ Ⓑ Ⓒ Ⓓ Ⓔ   43 Ⓐ Ⓑ Ⓒ Ⓓ Ⓔ   68 Ⓐ Ⓑ Ⓒ Ⓓ Ⓔ   93 Ⓐ Ⓑ Ⓒ Ⓓ Ⓔ
19 Ⓐ Ⓑ Ⓒ Ⓓ Ⓔ   44 Ⓐ Ⓑ Ⓒ Ⓓ Ⓔ   69 Ⓐ Ⓑ Ⓒ Ⓓ Ⓔ   94 Ⓐ Ⓑ Ⓒ Ⓓ Ⓔ
20 Ⓐ Ⓑ Ⓒ Ⓓ Ⓔ   45 Ⓐ Ⓑ Ⓒ Ⓓ Ⓔ   70 Ⓐ Ⓑ Ⓒ Ⓓ Ⓔ   95 Ⓐ Ⓑ Ⓒ Ⓓ Ⓔ
21 Ⓐ Ⓑ Ⓒ Ⓓ Ⓔ   46 Ⓐ Ⓑ Ⓒ Ⓓ Ⓔ   71 Ⓐ Ⓑ Ⓒ Ⓓ Ⓔ   96 Ⓐ Ⓑ Ⓒ Ⓓ Ⓔ
22 Ⓐ Ⓑ Ⓒ Ⓓ Ⓔ   47 Ⓐ Ⓑ Ⓒ Ⓓ Ⓔ   72 Ⓐ Ⓑ Ⓒ Ⓓ Ⓔ   97 Ⓐ Ⓑ Ⓒ Ⓓ Ⓔ
23 Ⓐ Ⓑ Ⓒ Ⓓ Ⓔ   48 Ⓐ Ⓑ Ⓒ Ⓓ Ⓔ   73 Ⓐ Ⓑ Ⓒ Ⓓ Ⓔ   98 Ⓐ Ⓑ Ⓒ Ⓓ Ⓔ
24 Ⓐ Ⓑ Ⓒ Ⓓ Ⓔ   49 Ⓐ Ⓑ Ⓒ Ⓓ Ⓔ   74 Ⓐ Ⓑ Ⓒ Ⓓ Ⓔ   99 Ⓐ Ⓑ Ⓒ Ⓓ Ⓔ
25 Ⓐ Ⓑ Ⓒ Ⓓ Ⓔ   50 Ⓐ Ⓑ Ⓒ Ⓓ Ⓔ   75 Ⓐ Ⓑ Ⓒ Ⓓ Ⓔ   100 Ⓐ Ⓑ Ⓒ Ⓓ Ⓔ

7 TEST BOOK SERIAL NUMBER (Copy from front of test book.)

8 BOOK CODE (Copy and grid as on back of test book.)

9 BOOK ID (Copy from back of test book.)

Quality Assurance Mark

Chemistry *Fill in circle CE only if II is correct explanation of I.

	I	II	CE*		I	II	CE*
101	T F	T F	○	109	T F	T F	○
102	T F	T F	○	110	T F	T F	○
103	T F	T F	○	111	T F	T F	○
104	T F	T F	○	112	T F	T F	○
105	T F	T F	○	113	T F	T F	○
106	T F	T F	○	114	T F	T F	○
107	T F	T F	○	115	T F	T F	○
108	T F	T F	○				

FOR OFFICIAL USE ONLY				
R/C	W/S1	FS/S2	CS/S3	WS

Page 4

PLEASE DO NOT WRITE IN THIS AREA

SERIAL #

23459 College Board 15b-10820-Text

Show up ready on test day.

There are over 20 videos to watch covering lots of biology topics. These lessons are great refreshers to help you get ready for the Biology Subject Test. And, you can also access video lesson playlists for Chemistry and Physics.

Disclaimer: Playlists were created based on videos available on Khan Academy. The contents are subject to change in the future.

Want **free** online lessons from Khan Academy®?

Check out **satsubjecttests.org/biology**.